A CHURCH FOR
THESE TIMES

A CHURCH FOR THESE TIMES

Ronald E. Osborn

1368

ABINGDON PRESS   *New York   Nashville*

A CHURCH FOR THESE TIMES

Copyright © 1965 by Abingdon Press

Library of Congress Catalog Card Number: 65-14720

SET UP, PRINTED, AND BOUND BY THE
PARTHENON PRESS, AT NASHVILLE,
TENNESSEE, UNITED STATES OF AMERICA

TO MY MOTHER

who loves the church and
who taught me to love it

ACKNOWLEDGMENTS

In January, 1964, it was my privilege to present the McFadin Lectures at University Christian Church, Fort Worth, under the auspices of Texas Christian University. The substance of chapters 2-4, 7, and 8, as well as some of the material in chapters 1, 5, and 6, was presented in those lectures. I am grateful to President M. E. Sadler for the honor of the invitation and for his hospitality. Dean Elmer D. Henson of Brite Divinity School and Granville T. Walker, minister of University Church also acted as gracious hosts; they extended many kindnesses, as did my longtime friend, Robert D. Chambless of Trinity Christian Church, Dallas. Albert C. Outler of Perkins School of Theology, Southern Methodist University, shared as Oreon E. Scott Lecturer along with Dr. Walker and myself, in the program of Ministers Week. Conversations with all the persons here named, and with many of the ministers from over the Southwest, were most profitable in the development of my thinking on various problems in this book.

Late in the same month I was guest of the Christian Ministers

7

of Florida for their annual retreat at Silver Springs, presenting again the material already indicated. To Lawrence M. Ashley, executive secretary of the Florida Christian Missionary Society, and to Mr. and Mrs. Earl W. Scarbeary of Central Christian Church, Orlando, I am grateful for hospitality. Three of my former students, Claire E. Berry (chairman of the program committee), Joseph Herndon Bragg, Jr., and R. Woody Kent, engaged in extended conversations concerning the issues; and the entire group of ministers participated in some animated periods of discussion which were helpful to me.

The Cornerstone Class at University Park Christian Church, Indianapolis, of which my wife and I have been co-teachers for some years, spent several Sundays on these chapters, and I am grateful to the members for their help.

To my colleagues on the faculty of Christian Theological Seminary and in the deliberations of the Consultation on Church Union who have read the draft and offered comments, I express my thanks, especially to Calvin L. Porter, Keith Watkins, and Don R. Wismar of Christian Theological Seminary and to Paul A. Crow, Jr., of Lexington Theological Seminary. Finally, I have received helpful and encouraging suggestions from my father, G. Edwin Osborn, distinguished professor-emeritus of preaching and worship in the Graduate Seminary, Phillips University. The errors which remain are my own.

Special thanks are due to my secretary, Mrs. Richard Tice, and to Miss Evelyn Hale, coordinator of secretarial services at Christian Theological Seminary, for help with the manuscript. I am particularly grateful to my friend and colleague, Henry K. Shaw, for making the index.

FOREWORD

A full generation ago William Temple, then Archbishop of Canterbury, called the ecumenical movement "the great new fact of our era." In those good old days before World War II few men could appreciate the significance of his words. And since then the world has seen the new facts of the space age, atomic power and other truly revolutionary forces. Yet today William Temple's words, I believe, have meaning for any reader of the daily press in which church councils have become newsworthy.

Scientific advance and worldwide revolutions make ever more dangerous the diversities and barriers among the peoples of the earth. But the humble man of goodwill and peace can be hopeful in the even greater new fact that a spiritual force is manifestly at work, crossing boundaries both old and new, and witnessing a oneness in Jesus Christ among all sorts and conditions of men, including ancient divisions within Christianity itself. Today the World Council of Churches, only a dream in William Temple's day, unites in Christian activity and intimate association Orthodox Christians of communist Russia and Pentecostal Christians from the population explosion of Latin America. And, at the same time, the Vatican Council is opening more and more associations, both personal and theological, between Roman Catholics and those now recognized as their separated brethren. From the uttermost parts of the earth and across backyard fences, new relationships in Christ considered impossible only a few short years ago now come into being daily.

It is in the light of this new situation, this miracle of precedent-shattering spiritual force, that Dean Ronald E. Osborn is led to address his "open letter to American Christians," which is the way he describes this little book. I have read the "open letter" before its general mailing and found my delight growing with each succeeding page. It is a little book in physical size, but it is big indeed in vision. And it packs an amazing amount of information and inspiration into an easily read and comprehended package.

And such a book is needed. All Christians are affected by the ecumenical movement, caught up and moved by its revelations, relationships, and forces. All read about church councils and are aware, favorably or unfavorably, of their activities. But few understand the real meaning of the councils and less believe, as I do most surely, that God himself is at work here in a reconciling and saving way. The great need is for more conscious participation, less resistance to inevitable change, more joyful expectancy on the part of ordinary Christians who have always believed that Jesus Christ was the hope of the world. Dean Osborn helps to fill that need.

My personal delight with this timely "open letter to American Christians" was enhanced by the gracious invitation to write this foreword. There is at least a little symbol of ecumenicity and the vision of Christian oneness when the Dean of a Christian Churches (Disciples of Christ) Seminary wants a Bishop of the Episcopal Church to introduce his book to be printed by a Methodist publishing house. And even that interdenominational project is only part of the symbol. Dean Osborn and I have become Christian friends and ecumenical colleagues because of our participation in the Consultation on Church Union, which important venture is the direct fruit of a challenging sermon preached by a Presbyterian, Eugene Carson Blake.

The basic theme of the book comes from the avowed purpose of the Consultation on Church Union, and of Dr. Blake's sermon —the search for a united church "truly catholic, truly reformed, and truly evangelical." These great characteristics of the church are explored by Dean Osborn in a most comprehensive and informative way. Surely all who call themselves Christians should manifest these marks of the church's nature, but the ideas behind the words have been narrowed by the divisions in the Christian body. It is one of the high values of this book that the author has acquired an interdenominational vocabulary and will thus lead any reader out of his own denominational narrowness of language.

Few, if any, of us fully appreciate how often our separations are perpetuated and deepened by the simple fact that we are not familiar with our separated brother's words. I, who call myself a catholic as well as a protestant, rejoice to find Dean Osborn writing in a "truly catholic" way, which may sound quite shocking to those of his tradition. It may be even more shocking, but I rejoice that Dean Osborn can quote Alexander Campbell, the spiritual father of the Disciples of Christ, in justification of Anglican pronouncements on the essentials of Christian unity.

But now enough of my ideas about it. You must read the book, and read it through to a surprise ending. For those in the six churches in the Consultation on Church Union the author has a special message, as he says, for Every Member, Every Young Person, Every Minister, Every Seminarian, and Every Official. That means about twenty million people and it would be appropriate to the author's high vision if the book were to win that many readers. And more, he has a word of challenge for "Every Christian in All the Churches" and for "Every Outsider," which takes in the whole world for which he longs to bring the Lordship and reconciling love of Jesus Christ.

Robert F. Gibson,
Bishop of the Diocese of Virginia,
Chairman of the Consultation on Church Union

12

CONTENTS

13

PART IV
A Church Truly Catholic

PART V
An Appeal for Faithful Obedience

INTRODUCTION
A Plea to American Christians

This book is an open letter to American Christians.

The voice of Jesus Christ has called us into his church. In this company of faith our destiny is to express the love of God by service to our fellowman.

All of us owe much to the church, not only as Christians but as inheritors of Western civilization, a way of life shaped to a remarkable degree by the labors of churchmen who have gone before us.

Yet today many are troubled about the church. Persons outside its membership think of it as having little regard for their real concerns. Those who struggle for justice or civil rights often feel that the church is no help to them, perhaps even has no desire to help. Within the church a rising chorus of voices charges that its witness is irrelevant and inconsequential. Young people offering themselves for the ministry find difficulty in accepting the traditional pastoral

15

role: They think they would like to be college teachers of religion, or hospital chaplains, or campus ministers. The church is the stumbling block. Morale among ministers themselves, we are repeatedly told, is low. Despite the outward signs of institutional success and material prosperity, the suspicion nags that nothing really crucial is happening. A friend of mine wryly expressed this uneasiness when I first visited the new church to which he had come to minister. "Welcome to the club," he said.

This book is written in the faith that God wills a church sufficient to the needs of these times. My effort is to catch a vision of such a church and to share it with you. Therefore I am determined to resist the temptation to write another extended account of the church's failures in our generation. You and I know them well enough, but we are bound to the lordship of Christ, who loved the church and gave himself up for her. Here too must be our love and our self-giving.

What then is the cause of our weakness? I offer no complete diagnosis, but speak of one dreadful ill which is visible at two points. The illness is *introversion,* a preoccupation of the church with itself. It may be seen both inwardly and outwardly.

Inwardly, in the realm of the spirit, the church has become deaf to the gospel. In eras of the church's power, elation at the good news of God is its dynamic force. Joy in the everlasting mercy charges the atmosphere of worship and weaves bonds of fellowship among all the believers; eagerness to proclaim the divine love turns the church outward in mission and in service. But when the gospel is muted, for whatever reason, the church degenerates into an institution for worthy purposes, a society for the cultivation of serenity, an organization of the "nice people." Only when the realization of God's love for us stirs us to our depths can we be saved from introversion. That is why a crucial section of this book deals with the gospel. The church must be transfigured.

16

Outwardly, as an institution, the American church has been terribly victimized by the excesses of the denominational system. Indeed, to speak of "the church in America," as I have been doing thus far, calls for a great labor of imagination on the part of the reader. What we have, in fact, is *churches,* a bewildering number and variety of them. And for all the gentlemanly behavior and Christian courtesy we can muster, denominations are in competition with one another. Each tends to become preoccupied with its own "success." Too often even "mission" itself becomes a self-serving device to build up the denomination rather than a response of love to the needs of men.

Largely because the denominational crazy-quilt reveals so inadequately the wholeness of the church, local congregations in America are weak in their understanding of what it means to belong to the universal Christian fellowship. They tend to become self-satisfied clubs of like-minded people in competition with people in other clubs like their own. So the institutional form of the American church exaggerates the introversion brought on by its spiritual deafness to the gospel. In order that the church may be delivered from its self-centeredness to the fulfillment of its true mission under God, one concern of this book is with freeing us from the extremes of the denominational system. Only by ending the folly and sin of meaningless division will the church in America find strength equal to her task.

The three major sections of this book direct our attention to God's will for the church as expressed in phrases freighted with meaning:

> *A church truly evangelical*
> *A church truly reformed*
> *A church truly catholic.*

Such a vision of the church is indeed my primary concern. And for the sake of the church's health I appeal to all earnest Christians to think seriously upon these topics.

It is obvious to the well-informed that these three phrases are associated with a particular movement in American Christianity today. The Consultation on Church Union is seeking a basis of union among six major denominations as a ground for a church truly catholic, truly reformed, and truly evangelical. I am a member of that Consultation, committed to the mandate which has been laid upon it. Yet this book is not conceived as a brief for a particular scheme of union; indeed, no scheme has yet been developed. Any presentation of such a plan must be preceded by widespread reflection on the part of American Christians concerning the nature of the church. And such reflection, followed by eager obedience to Christ as Lord, should result in spiritual renewal, whatever may be the fate of a particular program for union.

The responsible involvement of many believers in these concerns is the important issue now. In writing this "Plea to American Christians," I cannot help being mindful of the "Address to the German Nobility" which Martin Luther published at a crucial juncture of the Reformation. In 1520 the fate of reform depended, humanly speaking, on the decision of the Christian princes. Is it not true now that the fate of the church in America rests, humanly speaking, on the understanding and obedience of those earnest Christians who are its solid strength throughout the land? Spiritual renewal cannot be "programmed down from the top" of our denominational organizations. Nor can the reunion of the church be achieved just by sending our ecumenical specialists off to a few more conferences at delightful summer resorts (or even on the campuses of theological seminaries). The people of the churches must become involved.

This "Plea to American Christians" is written humbly, with no illusions of self-importance. The author is a workaday minister of the gospel convinced of the glory of our Lord's intention for his church and confident that his Spirit is at work among his own.

18

To invite all who have read thus far to sincere reflection on God's calling to the church in our land I have written the succeeding pages. The intent is to be reasonable and practical, not to argue so much as to explain, to reveal authentic emotion of Christian involvement without trying to move the reader by appeals to sentiment. I trust that you may read these pages thoughtfully and with a ready heart. Then pray, if you will, that God may grant us, and prepare us to receive, a church sufficient for these times.

PART I
A Vision of Christ's Church

CHAPTER 1
Towers in the Light

We may well be living in the golden age of American architecture. The long-sustained prosperity of our nation, the burgeoning population, the steady growth in productivity have combined to make this a period of unprecedented activity in major construction. Factories, office buildings, schools, churches, apartment houses, private dwellings rise to alter every familiar landscape. While much is "ticky-tacky," there is a satisfying proportion of distinguished buildings which will be a source of pride for years to come. These are the triumphs of our architects.

Across a period of more than five years it was my privilege to meet for repeated conversations with Edward Larrabee Barnes of New York, architect for the new campus of Christian Theological Seminary. It has been fascinating to watch a man of creative genius in the development of such a project. Architecture is at once the

23

grandest and the most mundane of the arts, calling for aesthetic vision and scientific expertise, for sensitivity of spirit and for a realism that remembers broom closets and plumbing. We watched the mind of our architect work—learning to know us and the spirit of our school, mastering the details of our projected requirements, mentally adapting the requisite bulk of the buildings to the peculiar contours of our site, trying one solution and then another to a particular problem, at last feeling his way through to the profile of the structure that would be. That last step was critical; indeed, it determined the character of the buildings. And everything that followed—the drawing of preliminary sketches, the drafting and redrafting of working drawings, the approval of the basic plans, the production of blueprints, the writing of specifications, the invitation for contractors' bids, the approval of a contract, the long work of construction, the progress toward dedication and occupancy —all this was determined by the architect's creative vision. That vision sustained everyone involved in the great effort of building.

This is the picture which Purd Dietz suggests in his well-loved hymn:

> Teach us to build; O Master, lend us sight
> To see the towers gleaming in the light.[1]

The purpose of this chapter is to suggest a vision of Christ's church which may serve like that of the architect. The mental image of those towers in the light can thus guide our labors as we seek from God a church for these times.

I

Fortunately we do not have to begin *de novo*. For a generation now the focus of Christian attention has centered on the church. The best minds of the ecclesiastical world have been wrestling with

24

the issues with which we must deal. The event may well prove that Providence has long been at work to enable the building of a church sufficient to these times. Perhaps no previous generation of Christians has given so much careful thought to the will of God for his church.

The men who went before us in the faith centered their interest or devotion on other objects. In the early centuries of our religion, Christians proudly accepted the glory of martyrdom. They looked for a reward laid up in heaven, gladly exclaiming "Thanks be to God!" when sentence of death was pronounced on them for the testimony of Jesus.[2] For a thousand years pious monks cultivated the mystical love of Christ, crying with the bride in Canticles: "I sought him whom my soul loveth."[3] These past four and a half centuries thousands of Protestants have sighed with the psalmist "O how love I thy law!" (Ps. 119:97, KJV) and dared to affirm with Martin Luther, *sola scriptura*—"The Bible alone!" Across the nineteenth century marched armies of idealistic believers singing "Let us die to make men free," or "Bring them in," or "De brewer's big hosses can't run over me," or "O Zion, haste, thy mission high fulfilling."

By the relatively recent days of my own youth we were singing "No more war!" In those romantic years when we saw ourselves as "Christian Youth Building a New World" our leaders often sounded apologetic about the church, or at any rate, confused. Its justification, if any, was instrumental, building the kingdom of God. But unfortunately the church did not seem to be a very effective instrument, divided as it was by the stultifying legacy of denominationalism and preoccupied with differences over theology and liturgy and other concerns which seemed irrelevant at the time.

(Nothing said here intends, of course, to leave the impression that no one before our day was interested in the church. We must not forget Augustine of Hippo, Leo the Great, Gregory the Great,

Innocent III, or Boniface VIII who uttered those ambiguous words: "Outside the church there is no salvation." Nor should we forget Calvin and Cranmer, the Puritans and the Tractarians. We should remember Bishop Frederic Dan Huntington, the Mercersburg theologians, Alexander Campbell and the Disciples, D. S. Warner and the Church of God, and many others. But to oversimplify, it is fair to say that the churchly concern of the great popes listed above was essentially institutional and that once the crisis of the Reformation was passed, issues pertaining to the nature of the church seldom commanded a priority of interest among pastors, theologians, and ecclesiastics throughout the generality of Christendom.)

How unexpectedly the men of my generation found our attention shifting to ecclesiology. That very word itself has taken on new meaning. A poor newspaper reporter heard it dropping from every lip at Lund, Sweden, during the Third World Conference on Faith and Order in 1952. He looked it up in the dictionary (so we were told) to find that it meant the study of ecclesiastical art and antiquities, with special reference to the adornment of churches. But to us today ecclesiology means the doctrine of the church. And we can almost date the self-conscious emergence of major concern for the church with the Oxford Conference of 1937.

By a gentle irony the 1937 meeting in Oxford was a Universal Christian Conference on Life and Work, the second such to be held. But the idealistic delegates who sailed away to England—passengers were not yet flying the Atlantic in those days—to speak with a united Christian voice on social problems walked down the gangplank into the freezing reality of a hard and bitter world. No gentle and gratifying session to improve society by pious and enlightened resolutions could be held any longer. The German delegates were missing, forbidden to attend, some of them held prisoners by the Nazis. (No ecumenical conference since that time has been complete, for in every instance at least one hostile government has cut off its Christians from meeting with their fellows.) Before the evil incarnate in Hitler that summer of 1937 the fragile dreams of a new and nicer world faded into thin air. The sudden shock of cold realism startled Christians generally into pondering anew the meaning of our corporate vocation in a dark and sinful world. And the call sounded at Oxford put iron in the blood of Christians everywhere: *"Let the church be the church."* Here was a fellowship of committed believers whose primary duty, whether the world proved hostile or friendly, was "to witness for God, . . . proclaiming the Will of God as the supreme standard to which all human wills must be subject and all human conduct must conform." Futhermore, "the primary duty of the Church to the State is to be the Church." [4]

Following upon action by the Oxford Conference, the World Council of Churches was soon in process of formation, a tentative condition which persisted until postwar 1948 and the historic constituting assembly at Amsterdam. Within fourteen years the World Council had become a fellowship of churches bridging the chasms of ancient ecclesiastical and modern political hostilities, embracing Russian Orthodox and Chilean Pentecostals, and including virtually every major communion except the Roman Catholic and Southern Baptist. It can be argued that a major factor in bringing on Vatican Council II has been the existence of the World Council of Churches. These two colorful phases of the ecumenical movement, the Roman and the non-Roman, have brought the dramatic reality of the worldwide church to the attention of mankind and have set the best minds of Christendom to thinking about the church's nature. New and unexpected miracles of reconciliation are continually happening, like the meeting of Pope Paul VI and the Greek Orthodox Patriarch Athenagoras on the Mount of Olives early in 1964.

Equally miraculous, if not always so dramatic, has been the conciliar movement in our more immediate communities, with the impressive growth of local, state, and national councils of churches. While few of the councils yet possess the strength their friends desire for them, their character is far richer than the practical co-operation in good works out of which they arose. Increasingly the councils are enlisting laymen and ministers in serious theological study concerning the nature of the church and its mission in the world.

The meeting of representatives from various denominations in ecumenical discussions has awakened among the individuals involved a keen awareness of the distinctive traditions from which the denominations come, prompting new theological and historical studies directed toward a reassessment of those peculiar emphases. The result has been a much more serious and responsible reflection on many issues of ecclesiology, eventuating in what promises to be the reformation of the denominations.

Vigorous programs of publication, conference, and discussion have ensued. Without benefit of heroics, manifestoes, marching songs, *autos-da-fé,* or other theatrical props, reformation is coming to more than one American communion.

II

Such widespread discussion concerning the nature of the church has led to growing uneasiness about the multiplicity of denominations in the United States—222 Protestant bodies according to the most recent count by the National Council of Churches. Considerably before Oxford, 1937, American churchmen had begun to be troubled by the inefficiency and irrelevance of so many separate communions. Despite the alleged bondage of ecclesiastical bureaucrats to their vested interests, the innate conservatism of religious institutions, and the difficulty of creating sentiment for change in democratically governed churches, a notable series of church mergers has occurred in the past forty years on this continent. Some of the more important bodies coming out of these are the United Church of Canada (1925), the Congregational-Christian Churches (1931), the Evangelical and Reformed Church (1934), The Methodist Church (1939), the Evangelical United Brethren Church (1946), the United Church of Christ (1957), the United Presbyterian Church (1958), the American Lutheran Church (1960), the Lutheran Church in America (1962). These have all been successfully carried through; various other conversations proved unsuccessful or still continue. In the latter category are negotiations between the Methodist Church and the Evangelical United Brethren, slated for consummation in 1968 and conversations between the Christian Churches (Disciples of Christ) and the United Church of Christ.

While these several unions of two or three denominations have tended to reduce the total number of Protestant bodies and may slightly increase the efficiency of some ecclesiastical enterprises, many Christians have longed for a more daring, more inclusive, yet realistic venture at unity. In the past half century four major proposals for large-scale union have been advanced in America.

In 1918 the Conference on Organic Union, made up of representatives from nineteen denominations, authorized the drafting of the so-called Philadelphia Plan of Union. It envisaged a federation, The United Churches of Christ in America, which it was hoped would lead to organic union of the participating churches. The hope was not fulfilled.

In the 1940's E. Stanley Jones gained widespread popular support, though no official action was taken by denominations, for his Plan of Federal Union.

In 1949 representatives of eight major communions, watched by official observers from several other bodies, formed the Conference on Church Union. Out of its efforts emerged the so-called Greenwich Plan, a Plan of Union for a United Church, which was ardently championed by Ivan Lee Holt, C. C. Morrison, and others. Withdrawal of support by the two major participating denominations resulted in termination of the Conference in 1958.

All three of these plans attempted to bypass the traditional issues of faith and order over which the churches found themselves divided. As a consequence, some of the most earnest and ecumenically responsible critics of the Greenwich Plan maintained that it did not take seriously the doctrine of the church. Yet the response of hopeful enthusiasm for each of these plans indicated a widespread popular longing for a united church at the center of American Protestantism. The need was for someone to sketch more clearly and acceptably the outlines of a united church, to set the "towers gleaming in the light."

The stated clerk of the United Presbyterian Church, Eugene Carson Blake, did just that in his famous sermon, "A Proposal Toward the Reunion of Christ's Church," preached at Grace Cathedral in San Francisco, December 4, 1960.

III

I can recall no single sermon in my lifetime which received such coverage throughout the nation, in the daily press, in the weekly news magazines and picture magazines, and in religious periodicals. (Incidentally, I am encouraged to believe that the people generally are more interested in Christian unity than we sometimes assume. At least the editors and journalists regularly give this theme the biggest play of any religious story. Witness their coverage of Blake's proposal, their coverage of World Council and National Council activities, and their coverage of Vatican Council II. Some of the most incisive reporting on these events appears not in the religious journals, but in *The New Yorker, Time, Life, Newsweek,* and *Saturday Evening Post.*)

30

The main outlines of Blake's proposal should be indicated here. He said,

Led, I pray, by the Holy Spirit, I propose to the Protestant Episcopal Church that it together with the United Presbyterian Church in the United States of America invite The Methodist Church and the United Church of Christ to form with us a plan of church union both catholic and reformed on the basis of the principles I shall later in this sermon suggest. Any other Churches which find that they can accept both the principles and plan would also be warmly invited to unite with us.

In the sermon, Blake set forth the principles of reunion to be understood as catholic, which I shall suggest only by key sentences:

1. The reunited Church must have visible and historical continuity with the Church of all ages before and after the Reformation. This will include a ministry which by its orders and ordination is recognized as widely as possible by all other Christian bodies. . . .
2. The reunited Church must clearly confess the historic trinitarian faith received from the Apostles and set forth in the Apostles' and Nicene Creeds. . . . The tendency in some of the so-called free Churches to suppose that no belief, that no confession of the faith, was necessary has given way to a general recognition of the necessity of corporate and individual confession of Christian faith as against the secular, humanistic, and atheistic ideologies of our times.
3. The reunited Church must administer the two sacraments, instituted by Christ, the Lord's Supper (or Holy Communion, or Eucharist) and Baptism. These must be understood truly as means of grace by which God's grace and presence are made available to His people. . . .

Subsequently Blake outlined the principles regarded as reformed:

1. The reunited Church must accept the principle of continuing reformation under the Word of God by the guidance of the Holy Spirit. . . .

31

God speaking through the Scriptures, must be able to reform the Church from age to age. . . . The reunited Church must keep Word and Sacrament equally and intimately united in understanding and appreciation.

2. The reunited Church must be truly democratic in its government, recognizing that the whole people of God are Christ's Church, that all Christians are Christ's ministers even though some in the Church are separated and ordained to the ministry of word and sacrament. . . .

3. The reunited Church must seek in a new way to recapture the brotherhood and sense of fellowship of all its members and ministers. . . .

4. Finally the reunited Church must find the way to include within its catholicity (and because of it) a wide diversity of theological formulation of the faith and a variety of worship and liturgy including worship that is non-liturgical.[5]

Immediate results of the sermon included acclamation far and near, and excited discussion among the delegates to the Fifth Assembly of the National Council of Churches, which was then in session in San Francisco. Within less than five months, forty-seven presbyteries made overtures to the General Assembly of the United Presbyterian Church in favor of the suggestion. The 173rd General Assembly meeting in Buffalo in May, 1961, passed almost unanimously a motion implementing the proposal and designating a delegation of nine Presbyterians to enter into conversations with the other churches "to explore the establishment of a united Church truly Catholic, truly Reformed, and truly Evangelical." [6]

There is the vision of the towers gleaming in the light. Out of the history, both painful and glorious, of God's people, three great words emerge to guide the building of a church for these times. Though these words are not quite comfortably familiar to many Christians, each of them represents a vast area of essential churchliness which cannot be excluded from any responsible thinking about ecclesiology. In his epochal sermon at San Francisco, Blake indicated the essential meaning of both *catholic* and *reformed*. No church will be sufficient for our times which does not take with utmost seriousness both the continuing history of the people of God throughout the centuries and the major issues raised by the Protestant reformers. The word *evangelical* is even more ancient than the other two and was dearly loved of the early Methodist leaders. It means, of course, "pertaining to the gospel" or "conforming to the gospel" or, more essentially, "deriving from the gospel." While the thought is surely implied in the words *catholic* and *reformed,* it represents an imperative element in the shaping of the church's life. We may be grateful therefore that it was included by the General Assembly in its description of the united church.

The General Convention of the Protestant Episcopal Church met in September, 1961, and took affirmative action on the proposal from the United Presbyterian Church. Responsible persons proceeded with the necessary arrangements, and in April, 1962, the Consultation on Church Union was organized in Washington, D.C. It was originally constituted by representatives from the United Presbyterian, Protestant Episcopal, and Methodist churches, and from the United Church of Christ. At that meeting formal invitations were sent to churches actually engaged in union conversations with any of the four member bodies. Thus at the second meeting of the Consultation held in Oberlin, Ohio in March, 1963, and at the third meeting held in Princeton, New Jersey, in April, 1964, appointed representatives of the Evangelical United Brethren and Christian Churches (Disciples of Christ) were also present. These six communions now constitute the membership of the Consultation; its chairman is Robert F. Gibson Jr., Episcopal Bishop of Virginia, who in 1964 succeeded James I. McCord, President of

Princeton Theological Seminary; its executive secretary is George L. Hunt, minister of the Fanwood (New Jersey) Presbyterian Church, and its associate executive secretary Paul A. Crow, Jr., of Lexington Theological Seminary.[7]

IV

I firmly believe that through the action of his Holy Spirit God is working in our time great miracles of reconciliation in the life of his church. One need only to look to Geneva, to South India, to Moscow, to Rome, to Jerusalem to see again that thrilling sight when "the walls come tumblin' down." Some of us who have labored through the meetings of the Consultation cherish the faith that another such miracle may be in prospect. It is too early to predict the probable outcome of our efforts; we have been given grace to believe that the enterprise is not only right, but (within the good providence of God) even possible.

It is instructive to reflect for a time on such a possibility. Just before leaving for Oberlin I was presiding in chapel at Christian Theological Seminary. In inviting intercessions on behalf of the Consultation I tried to sketch its purpose in about thirty seconds; and when I suggested that it was a conference to work on a plan of union among six denominations which might result in a church "truly catholic, truly reformed, and truly evangelical" a ripple of involuntary and incredulous laughter passed over the congregation of divinity students and professors. When so briefly put, the vision seems fantastic. And yet we prayed.

Does not that paradox of unbelief praying for faith epitomize the church's situation today? Despite the limits which cold reason imposes on what we are prepared to believe is probable, we all know in our inmost being as Christians that a church to be truly the church must be truly evangelical, truly reformed, and truly catholic. These are the towers in the light. I propose that we look ear-

34

nestly at these divine imperatives for the church, that we ask what they mean in ideal terms, that we hold them in judgment over the life of our congregations and of the larger church as we know it, and that we reflect on the possibilities of their ampler realization in the fuller life of a church sufficient for these times. This book is not a systematic commentary on Blake's sermon, nor a formal apologetic for a particular scheme of union. It is an effort to see the towers.

My responsibility in the ensuing pages I conceive not so much a matter of exhortation as it is of proclamation. For the holiness of the church is no mere Platonic ideal, reserved in spotless perfection in the heavenly places, and knowable to us only as a dark and distorted shadow dancing uncertainly on the uneven walls of this cave of our earthly existence. As Christians we confess that the divine perfection of the church interpenetrates and is made manifest in the ambiguous realities of its life in history. All of us who have been nurtured in the things of Christ by our spiritual mother, the church, are bound to confess that in our own knowledge of her, for all her limitations, she has shown herself to us by the grace of God to be truly catholic, truly reformed, and truly evangelical.

Even through the haze of earthly imperfections we have seen the towers gleaming, with the light of God upon them. In quest of a clearer vision of such a church, we now press on.

PART II
A Church Truly Evangelical

CHAPTER 2
The Good News of God

The movement of our thought brings us first to consider the evangelical character of the church. *Evangelical* requires translation, and not simply because it is a Greek word imported into English. It is the adjective derived from *evangel,* the gospel, the good news. But what does that mean? Many of our contemporaries, and not all of them outside the church, will ask just such a question. Recall my observation in the Introduction that the church in America has in large measure grown deaf to the gospel.

What is this good news which the preachers talk about? Despite the warnings of Karl Barth (who insists that we must always begin with God as made known in Scripture, not with man), I will approach this question by way of our human condition. For we are human beings—self-contained, self-conscious, self-regarding creatures. Any news that we read or hear is meaningless to us until we can understand that it has something to tell us about ourselves.

I

What then of our life?

It is a marvelous gift which came to each of us, unasked, from outside ourselves.

It is joy—a child's song, a shout of triumph, a bright fire and a warm meal after a hard day's work, the sheer euphoria of animal existence.

It is beauty—silent stars throbbing in a desert sky, the sudden, graceful bound of a deer clearing an obstacle in its course, the sleek economy of line in a racing automobile, the soaring height of a thirty-story building.

Life is hope and possibility. When we listen to Beethoven's "Ninth" or to an inspiring teacher, or a good preacher; when we read Aristotle or Petrarch or Whitman; when we muse by firelight, our spirits fairly race as imagination projects what we would be and do. The images of self-fulfillment which we clearly see in these moments are not mere pipe dreams; they are moments of insight when we truly discern the wonder of our own potential as men. The possibilities we have described become the guiding stars for our achievement.

Our life is the longing for love. Apparently the deepest law of our being is the need to be needed by others—to know the sense of belonging, to command the esteem of our peers, to mingle all our hopes and dreams with those of one other till death do us part, to feel the hand of a child encircling our finger for support.

However rebellious or angry we, or anyone else, may be at our world, however we may repudiate particular goals or patterns of behavior as sentimental, or square, or unsophisticated, or naïve, still—if we are men at all—we value our life for its promise of joy and beauty and hope and love.

But our life is not what we would have it. We do not live in the Garden of Eden. For life weighs us down with weariness. It demands of us hard and often over-taxing struggle. It strikes us down with pain. And precisely because we love, it smites us with sorrow, leaving us stunned and numb, a bleak emptiness sobbing in our hearts. Of all this—the weariness, the struggle, the pain, the woe—we can perhaps tell ourselves that it is part of our human existence. Every generation of men has had to bear these burdens, and many have borne them gallantly. Indeed, it may be said, the very threat of these possibilities serves to enhance the intensity of man's joy and beauty and hope and love.

But the ambiguity of our lives presents us with even darker complications. Our hopes do not turn out in accordance with our intentions; *frustration* has become one of the most overworked words in our speech. Ask almost anyone in the professions, or almost any housewife, how things are going. The answer is always, "Busy. There's too much to do. I can never seem to get caught up." The demands of our way of life conspire with the drive of our ego to mock the potentiality we have seen within ourselves. We find ourselves increasingly ridden by anxieties and fears in an age of enlightenment which has banished the bogeyman we only half-believed in and given us instead a hydrogen bomb we know is there. Most of our worries, however, are not about the fate of humanity in general; they center in our own little worlds—our families, our jobs, the narrow communities where our power is exercised and our ambitions seek expression. Here we often find joy gone sour and beauty turned to ashes, hope frustrated and love distorted or transmuted into rivalry, envy, and hatred. The bitterness of our lot springs from the knowledge that we cannot blame all this on other persons, or on the world at large. The root of our misery rises from our own nature; in this respect we are like the heroes of classic tragedy, except that in our case we are not often heroic and hence not truly tragic, but only contemptible-miserable men that we are.

41

And death at the last. Soon or late, suddenly or haltingly, mercifully or painfully, death will call us all into the valley of the dark shadow. The chilling awareness of the coming negation of all that we are, the blacking out of all joy and beauty, the blighting of hope and love, freezes the heart of man. Can we not explain something of the shock of the late President Kennedy's assassination, the intensity with which it was felt by so many citizens, by seeing it as a cruel and unexpected reminder of the inevitability and finality of death? In a moment this brilliant and engaging man with all his energy, his fortune, and his power, the symbol of our corporate life as a people, was gone. Man is like the beasts that perish.

There is surely no need, in this generation of existentialism, to labor the ambiguity of man's life, the uncertainty of our most cherished values, the absurdity of our death. On every hand we are reminded of these things by our most stylish artists, musicians, poets, dramatists, and theologians. "Man's existential situation" is the first cliché one must master if he wishes to be regarded as informed on the campus or at the cocktail lounge. Absurdity, we are told, is the plight of contemporary man.

The one reservation I wish to enter is simply to take issue with the notion that there is something peculiarly contemporary about this realization of man's condition. We used to laugh at the adolescent who learned about sex and thought it was something his parents never heard of. Equally ridiculous is the self-styled sophisticate who has read a little of Kafka or Sartre and now believes that late twentieth-century man is unique in his emptiness and despair. Contemporary man knows nothing bleak about the human situation which sensitive men have not always known, and known existentially, unless perhaps we are able to see more clearly than the men of the past four or five generations the ambiguities of scientific progress and man's inability, however enlightened he may be, to cure his own condition.

42

But despair, emptiness, bitterness are not new. I read them as a college boy in the poetry of Edwin Arlington Robinson and Siegfried Sassoon. If the early John Steinbeck was not so chilling as Bertolt Brecht, Leonid Andreyev was more so. Start reading back through literature for what the poets actually said, not for what is now so thoughtlessly said about them. Arnold and Tennyson and Longfellow knew the bitterness of man's condition and were shaken by it as much as our moderns; Shakespeare saw a "way of life . . . fall'n into the sere, the yellow leaf," and Dante knew what it was to wander through the dark wood of middle age, striving for the distant peak but repeatedly thwarted by the bestial impulses of his own nature and the beastliness of society. You can read the vanity of man's life in the Roman moralists and the Greek dramatists, in Ecclesiastes and Homer, in Egyptian and Babylonian poets, on the most ancient parchments and the earliest inscriptions. The art of the current existentialists is simple proof of humanity, not of modernity. Despair is a condition of the mortal soul, not of a particular century.

II

Into this night of man's bleak despair, at a moment in historic time, shone a light of great gladness. The Event was of such commanding importance as a watershed of our Western heritage that we date our calendars from it. In the first century of the new era, the Christians broke triumphantly into the streets of imperial Rome. And there, where Cicero had complained so eloquently about the sad state of affairs, wringing his hands and crying, *O tempora! O mores!* these evangelists proclaimed "The time is fulfilled." It was a new day. At the climax of history, God had spoken to man through his Son. This was good news, gospel, evangel. It was a word addressed not to that time alone but to all times, for it spoke glad tidings to our human condition, to the troubled soul of mankind in whatever generation. And the word it spoke is the very existence of the church evangelical.

What was this evangelical message, this good news which the Christians brought to man in his desperate situation?

The words are so familiar to us now that we simply cannot hear them in either the strangeness with which they fell on the ears of the Roman world or the exuberant gladness with which the apostles proclaimed them. Hence our deafness. And yet what strange words they were.

This is the gospel: "that Christ died for our sins in accordance with the scriptures, . . . that he was raised on the third day in accordance with the scriptures" (I Cor. 15:3-4).

There is the essence of the good news that brought the church into being and with which the church confronts the world. The paradox comes in the two words: "Christ died." What begins as a message of hope seems immediately to fall into despair. And then before the sentence is done the paradox is reversed: "He was buried, . . . he was raised on the third day." Who then is this victor over death?

He is Christ.

Sometimes we feel sorry for ourselves because of our presumed difficulty in communicating the gospel to modern hearers, but that has always been a problem. What did that name Christ mean in the first century? We know it as the Greek form of the Hebrew Messiah, God's Chosen, his Anointed. But to the Gentiles who first heard it, it appeared to be a proper name; it sounded like their word for "smeared," for that is what it meant: rubbed with oil. Yet the manner of the preachers was such that this odd-sounding term came through as a title all sublime. This man of whom they spoke was indeed the Chosen One of the Eternal God, sent at this time of destiny to fulfill the ages-old divine purpose. The great deeds of this act of God were in accordance with the Scriptures, making his nature and his will known in full as he had already made them partially known to the Hebrews. (Their sacred writings in the Greek translation called the Septuagint were widely venerated in the ancient world as a testimony to the one God, creator of heaven and earth, to the highest level of ethical living, to the great deliverance he would send for his people.) Now, said the preachers, the Deliverer, the Christ has come. The new age of Messiah has dawned. "When the time had fully come, God sent forth his Son" (Gal. 4:4).

Here is paradox all over again. For who was this Christ, this Son of God? He was Jesus of Nazareth, a Jew who earned his living at skilled labor and never set foot outside his obscure corner of the world. For a few months he preached the coming of the divine kingdom and then was put to death. Strange theophany this, stranger than any ever devised in the imagination of man. If only we had the gift to see it as it was. For it was all so unprepossessing, so unnoticed except by the eyes of faith.

Recently someone asked me what I thought of the motion picture "Cleopatra." My answer was: "I'm glad that Hollywood did it for once to something besides the Bible." And then I wished that someone in Hollywood might someday have the wit and the courage to film the gospel story as it really happened.

That would mean showing Rome as it appears in "Cleopatra"— a wide screen as wide as the world the legions conquered; technicolor for the splendor of the provinces, the grandeur of the capital, the glory of the triumphs, the blood spilled in conquest and in spectacle; extravaganza for the virility of the troops, the orgies of the emperors, the wealth of the nations, the frenzy of the arena; stars to play the roles of men and women who strode the earth as demigods and shattered old customs to mold a greater history. Rome was everything "Cleopatra" shows it as having been, and more.

But then the producer should let us see the gospel as it happened in an out-of-the-way county on the edge of the desert: a little band of sailors and dockhands tramping the barren trails with their Teacher who lost himself among the poor. Don't let the director hire ten thousand extras to jam a technicolor screen like teen-agers mobbing the Beatles. Leave the poor as they were, a few ragged cripples and a blind beggar forgotten in the shadows by the side of the road, with Jesus unnoticed among them, while the proud and the important sweep by commanding the world's attention. When he teaches from the mountainside, don't turn it into the world's largest echo chamber crowded like the Cotton Bowl on New Year's Day, but let it be what it was—the poor folk from a few villages listening to their Teacher talk about God.

His trial was not a dazzling courtroom drama but a hearing before a small-bore politician, well-nigh the lowest man in the pecking order of provincial administrators. Except for Herod's temple and the Roman praetorium, the Jerusalem where Jesus died was a lot more like Dodge City than it was like Rome. Another week gone, another three men dead, and all the little people that had seen them die were back in their accustomed places. Rembrandt had the courage to sketch the gospel incidents that way. The figure of Jesus all but blends in with those of the persons about him, except for a quiet, inner light. It is not by razzle-dazzle theatrics, but by faith, that he is known to be Son of God.

So it was in Galilee. Not by the insight of their natural powers, not by flesh and blood, were men moved to confess him the Christ, the Son of the living God, who had emptied himself to share their life. After his Crucifixion, the same thing was true of faith in the Resurrection. There was no spectacular pageant of triumph over death to dazzle an unbelieving world into acknowledgment of the great miracle—only the conviction of his closest followers that he had appeared to them in the breaking of bread. And with this conviction came the assurance that his Cross had been indeed a part of God's reconciling purpose, that he had entered fully into our lot —our life, our labor, our sorrow, our suffering, our death—had triumphed over all, had brought life and immortality to light through the gospel.

The assurance of his followers' faith touched with radiance everything they said about the life of their Lord. My imagination has been stirred by a little book by Martin Dibelius, now out of print, entitled *The Message of Jesus Christ*. Following the principles of form-criticism, Dibelius gathered together from the gospels samples of the early preaching about Jesus and arranged them by types: the old stories, parables, sayings, the great miracle tales, and legends. To see each separate unit set off by itself under each of these categories brings insight into the power of the gospel. Ordinarily we encounter these materials crammed into huge lumps called chapters. In reading the separate units (or better, in listening with the ears of the imagination to hear the early preachers), two overwhelming impressions sweep over the reader: brevity and joy. In virtually every memory of Jesus, perhaps only a sentence that he spoke, a mere scrap recalling one of his deeds, the full meaning of the gospel now seems to reside.

III

This is the gospel, said the early preacher, "which you received, in which you stand, by which you are saved" (I Cor. 15:1-2). To his hearers and to us it is good news. The joy, beauty, hope, and love which we have known as natural men we now see to be the gracious gift of the creating God who made himself known in Christ. The weariness, the struggle, the pain, and the woe which we bear we see that he has borne too, with a quiet gallantry and a radiant good cheer which he also bestows on those who follow in his steps. Our frustration likewise he has known, and far more bitterly than we. And our sin? For this he died. In the conviction that God was in Christ reconciling the world to himself a host of Christians from his time to ours has found forgiveness, deliverance, and constraining love. As for our last enemy, "Death is swallowed up in victory.... Thanks be to God, who gives us the victory through our Lord Jesus Christ" (I Cor. 15:54, 57).

A strange-sounding tale, you say? No stranger to us than it was to Roman ears, or Greek, or Hebrew. No man can force another to hear this as good news. The word of the cross is "a stumbling-block to Jews and folly to Gentiles, but to those who are called, both Jews and Greeks, Christ the power of God and the wisdom of God" (I Cor. 1:23-24).

CHAPTER 3
The People of the Good News

"To those who are called"! We are brought in our consideration to *the evangelical community,* the people of the good news.

A church truly evangelical. This is what we find on every page of the New Testament: A community of believers called into being by the gospel, sustained by the gospel, manifesting the gospel in their common life, witnessing to it in their worship and preaching and conversation, commissioned to share it in word and deed with those still waiting outside the church, shaping their institutional life by the good news through which the community exists. So we must describe the church. And if description is not definition, it is the necessary prelude to definition: The people with the good news of God. Do we need any more?

How is the life of this people sustained? If the church which is truly church must be truly evangelical, what makes it so? I suggest three requisites of the evangelical character of the church: (*a*) preaching, (b) sacraments, (c) ethics. Toward what is its life directed? We conclude by a consideration of the evangelical mission.

I

First, preaching. The word about Christ, his death, burial, resurrection, becomes the glad tidings of new life when any man responds to it in faith. And how does this happen? "Faith comes from what is heard, and what is heard comes by the preaching of Christ" (Rom. 10:17). The life of the church truly evangelical derives from the preaching of the good news. An ordinary man who knows that despair, bitterness, and death have been trodden down by Jesus Christ stands unostentatiously before a company of believers and bears witness to his faith. And their lives in Christ are renewed. The miracle of the church's being continues. And the longing doubter, the wretched sinner, the bitter outsider who hears is likewise granted the gift of saving faith. The doubter, the sinner, the outsider may be, as likely as not, a member of the church; he may be the preacher himself. For evangelism, proclaiming the good news, is needed everywhere, beginning with the house of God. Thus faith is restored. Surely the Protestant reformers were correct when they insisted that the true church is a church in which the gospel is rightly preached.

And what of the churches you and I know? For despite the dependence of the church for its very being upon the gospel, the preaching of the good news is often tragically muted. There have been bleak periods in the history of the church when men forgot how to preach—the Dark Ages (fitting name!) or the early eighteenth century in England, for example. And must we not say that the great eras of Christian glory have accompanied a flowering of preaching? Think of the fourth century when the largest men in the whole culture stood in Christian pulpits—Basil, the Gregorys, Chrysostom, Ambrose, Augustine. Think of the late Middle Ages and the tireless work of the wandering friars in bringing the gospel to the people—Francis of Assisi, Dominic, and a host of eloquent followers. Think of the Reformation—the thunder of Luther, the scholarship of Calvin, the broadsword that was Knox. Think of the eighteenth century, when the Church of England had grown proud and cold, with George Whitefield and John Wesley preaching forgiveness at the mouths of the mines and in the fields, and Charles Wesley crying, "O for a thousand tongues!" I think of the days of my own youth, when in the pulpits of the Disciples I heard men like A. E. Cory, Raphael H. Miller, S. Lee Sadler, Peter Ainslie, George Hamilton Combs, Edgar DeWitt Jones, J. Warren Hastings, and Clarence E. Lemmon. What of today?

One of my nephews is a graduate student in English at Harvard. At Christmastime, he spoke to me of "Lycidas," which his professor had characterized as "the greatest poem in the English language." The years had passed since I had read it; so I pulled it from the shelf. In it, Milton laments, under the form of a pastoral elegy, the death of his young friend drowned in the Irish Sea. (Edward King had been a divinity student.) After describing their happy life together as shepherds, a figure which the elegiac form demanded, Milton comes to the sorry state of the church in his day and the deprivation which the death of this dedicated theological student has brought not only to his friends but to the woebegone people of God. The poet introduces Peter as chief bishop to mourn the loss of a young shepherd so desperately needed:

> He shook his Mitred locks, and stern bespake,
> "How well could I have spared for thee, young swain,
> Enow of such, as for their bellies' sake,
> Creep and intrude, and climb into the fold!
> Of other care they little reckoning make,
> Than how to scramble at the shearers' feast,

51

And shove away the worthy bidden guest.
Blind mouths! that scarce themselves know how to hold
A Sheep-hook, or have learned aught else the least
That to the faithful Herdman's art belongs!
What recks it them? What need they? They are sped;
And when they list, their lean and flashy songs
Grate on their scrannel Pipes of wretched straw;
The hungry Sheep look up, and are not fed. . . .[1]

The lifeblood of the true church is the gospel, and men must be called to preach it with faithfulness and zeal.

A church sufficient for these times, a church truly evangelical, concerns itself with preaching. I am not pleading for a return to the theatrical oratory of our grandfathers' day which so easily rendered the preacher a pompous and ridiculous figure. The gaslit era is gone, and we no longer need its "pulpit giants." (Alas, the metaphor was too often true: Before the days of electronic amplification by public address systems the girth of a hippopotamus was one of the qualifications for oratory!) But the earnest witness of what God has done in Christ—spoken by a living voice to living hearers—remains the means of the church's life. And not only must the grace of God be proclaimed. The meaning of his action in Christ and of his continuing call to man must be spoken into the specific situations in which we live here and now. This is the essence of preaching.

What are the prospects for today's church at this point? They are encouraging. The liturgical movement has recovered a sense of the significance of preaching within the context of worship, and there are signs of a flowering of preaching in the Roman Catholic, the Protestant Episcopal, and the Lutheran churches. The great Protestant theologians of our day—preeminently Karl Barth—have been preoccupied with the theme, the Word of God, and think of the church's task as *kerygmatic* or proclamatory. Other leaders of

Christian thought—especially Paul Tillich and Rudolf Bultmann—have centered their attention on the *meaning* of the ancient Christian witness for contemporary man. Biblical scholars have emphasized the decisive role of preaching in giving form to our Scriptures. Thus in a theoretical way preaching has been given an importance in Christian thought which it has seldom enjoyed.

If the practice in many Protestant pulpits seems to fall short, there are explanations. Many of today's ministers received their education before the new emphasis was running strong in the seminaries. The younger men are perhaps hindered by a tendency now in vogue to speak in abstractions and in polysyllables. All are oppressed by the clamor of contemporary church life, with its constant round of meetings and activities, and with little time for study and reflection. Some laymen are so sensitive to any discussion of "controversial issues" and so quick to admonish the minister to confine his discourse to Bible times or to harmless spirituality that a few preachers have been either soured or broken. Yet despite all the difficulties, one can sense in almost any group of theological students or company of ministers a longing to proclaim the good news of God.

Preaching the Word with faith, the faith of people and minister alike, is an essential mark of a church truly evangelical.

II

The pure preaching of the gospel and the faithful administration of the sacraments are the reformers' marks of the true church. They rightly saw that the sacraments, like preaching, are given to the evangelical community to sustain its life by the proclamation of the good news.

Consider the mystery of baptism in the thinking of Paul. In this sacred rite the believer is united with Christ in a death like his in the assurance of likewise being united with him in a resurrection like his (see Rom. 6:5). Could we ask for any more striking demonstration of the way in which the gospel brings the church into being? We are a people incorporated into union with Christ in our baptism and so brought into union with all fellow believers. "By one Spirit we were all baptized into one body—Jews or Greeks, slaves or free" (I Cor. 12:13). As a sacrament of the gospel, baptism becomes the great proclamation of our unity in Christ. Hence the growing theological interest in this sacrament in ecumenical circles. For a church truly evangelical will understand and manifest the oneness of God's people whom he has called into being by the gospel.

Because of the oft-repeated words of institution, we are more accustomed to think of holy communion as a monstrance of the gospel—showing forth the Lord's death until he comes. The recent studies of Oscar Cullmann on *Early Christian Worship* have underscored the evangelical character of this sacrament as a witness to the Resurrection. It was "on the first day of the week," the day of resurrection, that the disciples "were gathered together to break bread" (Acts 20:7). In a remarkable way the whole sweep of the church's life, past, present, and future, was concentrated into this simple act of breaking bread together in the presence of the risen Lord. The crucial prayer in the earliest Christian liturgies is *Maranatha,* "Our Lord, come!" "This ancient prayer," says Cullmann, "points at the same time backwards to Christ's appearance on the day of his resurrection, to his present appearance at the common meal of the community and forwards to his appearance at the End, which is often represented by the picture of a Messianic meal." [2]

(One of the most suggestive developments in the current revival of liturgical theology in the Roman Catholic Church follows this early Christian way of thinking. Pioneered by European Benedictines at Maria Laach and disseminated in the United States by their brethren in the abbey at Collegeville, Minnesota, it is known

54

as the *Mysterientheologie*. In "the action memorial of the sacrifice of Christ" in the breaking of bread according to this point of view, the "past event becomes really present now. The very nature of a sacrament is this real presence of a past event in ongoing time."[3])

On a bright spring day a little group of us walked the ancient village pavement and entered the Latin church at the traditional site of Emmaus. I was at once struck by the appropriateness of the large mosaic depicting the beloved incident on the evening of the first Easter when the risen Lord was made known to the two disciples in the breaking of bread. Is this not the picture we should place above our communion tables rather than that of the Last Supper? And if Cullmann is right—I believe that he is—perhaps our interpretation of "the words of institution" should be broadened to include the accounts of the Resurrection-communions. In their meeting with the living Lord the life of the evangelical people is sustained.

The sacrament of holy communion becomes a powerful witness to the love of God, even under the most trying circumstances. One of the pioneers in the teamwork between religion and psych John Rathbone Oliver, an Episcopalian priest, has recoun coming to the mental hospital of some quiet "parson" carrying the consecrated host from the altar to poor su ward. He testifies that the ministry of our Lord's b left distraught patients strangely quieted and com every pastor could tell of similar experiences wit lirium. Bread and wine become a monstrance o

Contemporary man, swallowed up in our grea ters, is discovering anew the power of religious cially of symbolic actions to convey the depths o Our frontier ancestors meeting in their rude ch ance in the simple word of preaching or testi be embarrassed by ritual. Not only environmental circumstance but psychological necessity stripped their meetinghouses of ceremony and of symbol. Abetted by the inheritance of Puritanism, "American nonliturgical worship" persisted after the passing of the frontier, with its bare bones of hymn and scripture and extemporaneous prayer and sermon. But the sons of the pioneers who make up the "lonely crowd" in our great cities long for more than this. Worshiping in large congregations where they really know few persons around them, they find depths of meaning in the ceremonial acts which have come down as the Christian tradition. Such acts must be frequently interpreted, but once their meaning has been made clear they seem to have power to convey the assurance of divine grace below the level of language. A church truly evangelical shows forth the gospel through the action of the sacraments.

III

Let it never be forgotten that the life given to the community of the good news is indeed a new life. The ethic of the Christian life, both as gift and as demand, is part of the gospel.

nything made the early Christians distinctive from the followers of the other religions all about them, it was the way in which
devotion to the Christian Savior-God was linked with the
of a new way of living. Sinners were forgiven by
no merit of their own, but they were called to walk
And that newness was a genuine reality. Much
things from the pages of the New Testament is
n who have been picked up from a life of shame
the brightness and the warmth of the house-
hey are expected to live like members of his
the power to do so.

R. H. Strachan is pertinent here:

It is unfortunate that the term *kerygma*—"preaching"—has become in modern critical parlance a synonym for *euangelion* and tends to displace it. This fosters the idea that the "gospel" can be distinguished in thought from *didache* or moral teaching. The Christian catechumen at baptism made confession of faith in the words "Jesus is Lord" (Rom. 10:9). In so doing he bound himself to put into practice the teaching of his Lord (Matt. 7:21-23; Luke 6:46). Both by confession and by manner of life the Christian disciple is an evangelist.[5]

Strachan's observation is all to the point. How many unbelievers from the time of the apostles till our day have had their first hint of the good news of God in the uprightness of life of some humble disciple. None of our theological insights into the continuing hold of sin over every man or our constant need for confession should blind us to the transforming power of the redeeming Christ in the lives of his people. To read the great ethical sections in the epistles is to realize once again what men in Christ can become. And to find oneself in the company of God's people is to know a fellowship which both demands and sustains this quality of living. The new uprightness, like the preaching and the sacraments, is a proclamation of the gospel. The old Adam, the natural man of the sinful flesh is dead; the believer has been raised with Christ and his thoughts are set on the things that are above.

So by preaching, sacrament, and manner of life the people whom God has called into being by the gospel proclaim that gospel through the evangelical community and to the world.

IV

Yes, to the world. A true church, sufficient to these times, is committed to *the evangelical mission,* making known the good news.

While it is important for us as the people of God constantly to remember who we are, and thus to reflect in joy on the glad tidings by which God has called us into being, the Lord did not put his church in the world just to preach the gospel to itself. "The field is the world." Thus the imperative to mission. As the body of Christ the church is called to minister in his name to the needs of lonely, sorrowing, puzzled, embittered, and despairing men. Without zeal for its mission, the church cannot be truly evangelical. Indeed, it cannot even be the church.

The irony and failure of self-serving religion were scathingly portrayed by Archibald MacLeish in *J.B.*, his dramatic rendition of the story of Job in a modern setting. Do you remember the terrible moment of J.B.'s torment when his three "friends" descend upon him to "comfort" him? One is a Marxist, one a Freudian, and one a comfortable, self-centered incarnation of institutional religion, some kind of clergyman who utters pious clichés in unfeeling response to J.B.'s agony, and couldn't care less about the plight of the sufferer? Is this how the church looks to modern man? Is this a true measure of our sense of mission?

Whenever the chosen people of God become keenly aware of "the wonderful deeds of him who called [us] out of darkness into his marvelous light" we will respond to our calling "to declare" these "wonderful deeds" (I Pet. 2:9). Therefore the evangelical community must give attention to its institutions to determine whether or not they are really adequate to express the true nature of the church as a people called of God by the gospel to make that gospel known to all mankind.

Does the church as we know it in America help the world grasp the meaning of God's reconciling work in Christ? Can it see by the forms of our life that we are the reconciled people of God? What do our denominational separations say about the power of the gospel to break down hostility among men? What do our class churches say? What do our race churches say? What does our long estrangement from the Jews say? What does our aloofness from human misery say?

58

In ecumenical circles one of the creative studies now going on is concerned with the missionary structure of the congregation. I confess that some of the proposals being advanced in this study have not yet convinced me; for example, while I understand the radical changes that have occurred recently in our society with respect to the types of community in which men live, I am not yet ready to write off the parish church as irrelevant to contemporary man. I have some questions about it nevertheless. What picture of itself does our average congregation today get across to its typical member or to the neighbor who does not belong? Is it seen as a fellowship of love and service uniting its members in the fulfillment of their divine calling and eager to minister to the real needs of persons in the community it serves? Or does it give the impression of exploiting its members and the outsiders it would like to reach? Is its evangelism an earnest sharing of good news with men dying for lack of that word? Or is it a carefully calculated branch of salesmanship designed to build up the institution? Particularly in communities which suffer from being "overchurched," as we say, can we really clear ourselves of the charge of exploitation, devouring the sheep we were sent to feed? At such a very practical level in the fulfillment of our mission, a proposal for the reunion of Christ's church is particularly germane. Can a divided church be truly evangelical?

Sometimes the church presents itself to the world as being far more concerned with its heirlooms than with its mission. In Roman Catholicism, for example, many traditions have no connection with the Christian faith; they are vestiges of feudal custom, inherited from the church of the Middle Ages. They have hung on, like barnacles encrusting a ship, because they are familiar, and people resist change in religion. But the time comes when such meaningless remnants must be stripped away to free the church for its task. So Pope John XXIII proved his greatness as a pastor by issuing his call for *aggiornamento,* the updating of the life of the Roman Church, making it relevant to contemporary man.

As for our American Protestantism, its heirlooms are its more than two hundred denominations, inherited from the past in assorted shapes, sizes, colors, and descriptions, but none of them really designed to proclaim the gospel to our day. Antiques make interesting, sometimes even valuable, collectors' items. Aesthetic pleasure combines with pride of possession in the act of admiring a well-crafted apple butter kettle or ox yoke or oil lamp or churn. Yet who wants to live in a nineteenth-century house, with nineteenth-century furniture, using nineteenth-century implements? We admire our great-grandfathers for their resourcefulness, their intelligence, and a host of other commendable qualities, but we have to live our lives in our time. Does our typical American denomination with its hallowed "sense of tradition"—a tradition formed in the nineteenth century, or possibly the eighteenth—really bear any more vital relationship to our time than does a "one horse open sleigh"? We like this church tradition because it is ours, and its songs are fun to sing. But suppose we are not so concerned about quaintness as about witness?

A church truly evangelical is a church with a mission, a church which constantly seeks to make every aspect of her life an authentic means of declaring the good news.

V

We began our consideration of the church evangelical by pondering our human condition. We saw how the act of God in Christ addressed itself to our deepest needs. That good news is ours to declare, and all the world is waiting. Though it may not know what it awaits, in the loneliness of the night it knows its own misery. And though there are some who think that the gospel belongs to a day that is gone, they cannot conceal a longing to believe it.

We do believe. And our calling is to share the glad tidings that God is still at work among men.

Christopher Fry's drama *Thor, With Angels,* is set in pagan England in the year 596 when Pope Gregory the Great sends the monk Augustine to convert the kingdom of Kent. Merlin the legendary magician recalls the departure of the Roman legions long ago, the darkness and warfare which then descended upon the land like the cold of winter; and now he foretells the approaching hope of life which his gift of clairvoyance enables him to discern on the distant sea. Merlin is speaking:

> When, years ago,
> The Romans fell away from our branching roads
> Like brazen leaves, answering
> The hopeless windy trumpets from their home,
> Your tribes waged winter upon us, till our limbs
> Ached with the carving cold. You blackened
> The veins of the valleys with our dried blood. And at last
> Your lives croaked like crows on a dead bough
> And the echoes clanged against you. But I can hear
> Faintly on the twittering sea a sail
> Moving greatly where the waves, like harvest-home,
> Come hugely on our coast: the men of Rome
> Returning, bringing God, winter over, a breath
> Of green exhaled from the hedges, the wall of sky
> Breached by larksong. Primrose and violet
> And all frail privileges of the early ground
> Gather like pilgrims in the aisles of the sun.
> A ship in full foliage rides in
> Over the February foam, and rests
> Upon Britain.

The ship is an ancient symbol of the church. Whenever the ship bears the good news of God, that church is truly evangelical, bringing springtime to the wintry shore of man's life.

61

Ponder the line which one of the pagans speaks to a Christian as the missionaries arrive.

> Your god has come, perhaps,
> Or lies in wait on the lips of a man from Rome.[6]

We are the evangelical community, the people of the good news. And does God lie in wait upon our lips?

PART III
A Church Truly Reformed

CHAPTER 4
Servants of the Living Lord

A church sufficient for these times must be "truly reformed." Just what does this say? And why say it that way?

When paired with "truly catholic," the phrase "truly reformed" suggests, as it was doubtless intended to do, all that is valid and essential in the Protestant conception of the church.

There has been much popular misunderstanding at this point, for "Protestant" has too often been taken to mean "anti-Roman Catholic." In times past such anti-Roman bigotry has proved a highly explosive force in American society, but the fuse must have been dampened by the ecumenical rains, for it now seems slow to take the spark. John F. Kennedy, Pope John XXIII, and Cardinal Cushing have projected a new image of Roman Catholicism, no longer horrendous. So, who wants to make anything of being a Protestant? Today it is difficult to get anyone out to Reformation Day Rallies.[1] Some communities where such mass demonstrations of Protestant strength flourished only a few years ago have given them up altogether. To whatever degree popular Protestant loyalty ever took the form of anti-Roman antagonism, we welcome the change.

But it would be disastrous to conclude that the Protestant Reformation of the sixteenth century was a tempest in a teapot. Great issues were at stake, and both sides were contending for important concerns, as well as for lesser interests which no longer have relevance for us. The reformers saw themselves as witnessing positively to the Christian gospel, not just as leading a protest movement. They proclaimed the good news of God; they testified to the ancient faith; they loved the historic church. But they saw it standing constantly under the judgment of the Word of God.

That is the genius of any ecclesiology which affirms that the church must be truly reformed. It is not a matter of one great overhaul, cleaning up the institution in the sixteenth century. *Ecclesia reformata semper reformanda,* cried the heroes of Protestantism: The church which has been reformed is under necessity of continual reformation.

Such doctrine is in no sense partisan. Rome accepts it and vocally proclaims it through the writings of a whole generation of exciting young theologians. A great company of bishops, along with Pope John and Pope Paul VI have given their *imprimatur* to this concept. Like Protestantism and even Orthodoxy, Rome is being reformed in our day.

Indeed, the concept of a true church as being of necessity truly reformed is not a modern but a biblical idea. It is of the essence of the church to be constantly undergoing reformation, being made new, its secondary securities shattered, as it lives out its radical obedience to God in a changing world. Religious institution must continually be made over. Consider the experience of the prophet:

66

The word that came to Jeremiah from the Lord: "Arise, and go down to the potter's house, and there I will let you hear my words." So I went down to the potter's house, and there he was working at his wheel. And the vessel he was making of clay was spoiled in the potter's hand, and he reworked it into another vessel, as it seemed good to the potter to do.

Then the word of the Lord came to me: "O house of Israel, can I not do with you as this potter has done? says the Lord. Behold, like the clay in the potter's hand, so are you in my hand, O house of Israel" (Jer. 18:1-6).

Not very comfortable doctrine that! It is subversive of the security of religious institutions—but essentially biblical, typically prophetic, and constantly necessary.

Consider the even more violent metaphor used by an early Christian:

See that you do not refuse him who is speaking. For if they did not escape when they refused him who warned them on earth, much less shall we escape if we reject him who warns from heaven. His voice then shook the earth; but now he has promised, "Yet once more I will shake not only the earth but also the heaven." This phrase, "Yet once more," indicates the removal of what is shaken, as of what has been made, in order that what cannot be shaken may remain. Therefore let us be grateful for receiving a kingdom that cannot be shaken, and thus let us offer to God acceptable worship, with reverence and awe; for our God is a consuming fire (Heb. 12:25-29).

What cannot be shaken in the church will remain—what is truly evangelical, truly reformed, and truly catholic. But much in our churchly life does not qualify under those terms, indeed may even contradict them. Consequently the church in history constantly stands in the time of "Yet once more." The eternal God, who is ever the same, continually encounters us in new situations, demanding of us as his people new and radical obedience and calling for the reshaping of our religious institution. If the church is to be truly reformed, we must ever be alert for the voice of divine judgment, ever sensitive to those practices and attitudes in our ecclesiastical life which tend to deny the gospel, ever eager for the renewal of spirit which God bestows upon his faithful people. *Semper reformanda:* always being reformed.

Our attention to this theme will occupy three chapters: "Servants of the Living Lord," "The Church of the Biblical Witness," and "The Need for Recurring Reformation." In this chapter we consider the people of God as servants of the living Lord.

I

Sociologists tend to regard religion as a conservative institution within society. They see it as powerfully persistent and incredibly adaptable, to be sure, but backward-looking, invoking divine sanctions for the preservation of things-as-they-were and particularly for the church-as-it-was. Many believers think of it in the same manner. Hence the sanctification of holy memories. Hence the preservation of religious relics (whether they be bones of the martyrs, denominational traditions, or gospel songs). And hence the powerful appeal of "the old-time religion." We all understand this phenomenon, and to some degree we all participate in it.

Yet nothing could have struck the apostles as more incredible than the suggestion that their faith was centered in the past. It had roots in past experience, of course, just as does the meaningful life of each of our families. We love to recall the first date, the details of the wedding, the birth of the children, the clever things that they said and the escapades they got into when they were young. But if someone tells you in sociological terms that your family is to be understood as a conservative institution you respond that he does not really understand your family. It is a present relationship. This very day there are bills to pay and new shoes to buy and letters to write and problems to face together. There are shared joys. And there is love which is something far more than a beautiful memory or an incidental habit.

That is the meaning of the miracle of Easter and the miracle of Pentecost. Jesus of Nazareth is not just a precious memory lingering from days that are gone and will never be again; he is the living Lord. A biography of the man of Nazareth, no matter how accurate as history and how compelling as literature, simply cannot explain the life of the church. The Lord's supper kept as an act of symbolic remembrance, no matter how soul-searching and how inspiring, falls short of what believing Christians really mean by holy communion. The church of Christ striving to discern from a book just how something was done at Jerusalem or Antioch and trying to reproduce the procedure exactly as it was then is not the church of the New Testament. The church found its existence in the reality of a living power, the presence of him whom God has raised up and has made both Lord and Christ, this Jesus who was crucified. Thus the church continued the genius of its Master whose belief was not something to be proved from a book but a faith centered on the reality of the living God—the God of Abraham, Isaac, and Jacob, and of their seed, and hence Abba: Father. The central reality of our life in the church roots in the earthly career of Jesus, and thanks be to God for all that he was and said and did. But it comes to flower in the present encounter of the living Christ with the faithful: "Blessed are those who have not seen and yet believe" (John 20:29).

The vitality of the early church, its dynamic, its reformability—already its reformability—derive not from the forms of its life but from its continuing encounter with the Holy Spirit. Here was a company of people brought into being by the good news of God's gracious act in Christ, an act not only past but present, a people finding continual joy, power, excitement, and leading in the indwelling of the Spirit with them. To read the Book of Acts is to see, as Ph.-H. Menoud reminds us,[2] that its

chief personage ... is neither Peter nor Paul, but the Spirit, who makes the Church increase in number and vigour (9:31), who inspires the decisions necessary to maintain her unity (15:28), who guides the apostles and preachers of the Gospel in their missionary journeys (4:8; 6:10; 8:29; 10:19; 13:2-4; 20:23), who establishes the essential ministries (6:6; 20:28), who sends warnings by the prophets (11:28; 21:4-11). On this the Epistles of Paul confirm the evidence of Acts.

The amazing aspect of the Spirit's dealings with the church—especially if one holds the notion of religion as a conservative force or a static institution—is that the Spirit was constantly confronting the church with new demands. The church was being continually re-formed by the Spirit. It was by the Spirit's leading that the evangelist Philip was prompted to witness to an unknown Ethiopian. It was the Spirit who led the Apostle Peter to open the doors of the church to Gentiles. It was the Spirit who guided the Jerusalem council in its decision that the ancient and sacred ordinance of circumcision could no longer be held absolute within the church. It was the Spirit who turned the Apostle Paul away from his home country of Asia Minor and launched him on his mission to Macedonia and Greece and Rome. In short, it was the action of the Holy Spirit in the common life of the early church which prevented her from becoming a typical religious institution, backward-looking in her interests, static in her forms, exclusive in her fellowship, introverted in her concerns. It is the Spirit who continually reforms the church.

As the decades passed, the people of God gradually lost some of the spontaneity of their earlier life in the Spirit. As the church grew in size and became a familiar part of the landscape, at least to its members, fixed patterns of action became established. Christian institutions took form, claiming apostolic authority, under the leadership of an ordered ministry. The excesses of emotionally unstable believers who equated the presence of the Spirit with nervous excitement and irrelevant bodily activities led to revulsion among the better balanced and more rational members of the church. The claim of inspiration by the Holy Spirit on the part of those who advanced bizarre doctrines and practices not in harmony with the faith received from the apostles led to insistence on the part of the bishops that the Spirit works through the ordered life of the church rather than through the unbridled enthusiasm of undisciplined individuals. Any claim to spiritual gifts or to inspiration by the Spirit ultimately had to be submitted to the reverent judgment of the Christian community. The church is the final earthly arbiter of the spirits, testing whether they are of God. With such a contention we must surely agree; it is one aspect of the meaning of the church's being truly catholic. Yet the danger of order is a preoccupation with institution and procedure and prerogative. The satisfaction of proper protocol replaces the joy of life in the Spirit. Faithfulness then becomes a matter of upholding tradition rather than of freely seeking the will of the Lord in a new situation.

The Spirit-led church of the apostolic generation was not a church without norms. She derived her very being from the redemptive act of God proclaimed in the gospel, and her total life was lived out under the lordship of Christ. The leading of the Spirit offered no threat of departing from the gospel; rather it was the gracious gift of the living Lord which enabled the church to understand the obligations of living under the gospel in each new situation. "No one speaking by the Spirit of God ever says 'Jesus be cursed!' and no one can say 'Jesus is Lord' except by the Holy Spirit" (I Cor. 12:3).

71

II

Only the slightest work of "demythologizing" (translating ancient modes of religious expression into modern thought-forms) is necessary, I believe, to discern in the experience of the apostolic church with the Holy Spirit a proper understanding of the church's obedience in every generation. Year by year and in constantly unexpected ways the Lord of history confronts his people with new and unprecedented situations. How do we determine a Christian course of action? There is for us no Urim and Thummim, no oracle of Delphi. The books of the New Testament, brief and precious as they are, make no pretense of containing a prescription for every contingency in Christian history. The people of God must seek the leading of the Spirit. And what does this mean? It means mutual consultation in the community of Christian love. It means corporate reflection on God's saving act in Jesus Christ made known to us in the gospel. It means hard thought as various individuals express their convictions, their questions, and their tentative answers clearly, firmly, and unpretentiously in the manner of James and Peter and Paul at the Jerusalem council. It means prayerful and eager seeking, not for the triumph of our own special line, but for the gift of one heart and a new spirit which God promises to his people (see Ezek. 11:19). It means grateful new steps in obedience when a common mind is obtained.

There is nothing startling or original in this analysis. The apostolic church, the Eastern Orthodox Christians, the English Puritans, the Society of Friends, and many a modern congregation among the free churches know this procedure. It has provided the pathways to fuller understanding in ecumenical encounter although we must confess that many issues among Christians still remain unresolved. Our earnest seeking of the Spirit's guidance is not so much a matter of finding ready answers to the church's questions as of constant effort to keep the spirit of the Christian community in tune with the will of God. To be led by the Spirit, we must cultivate spiritual sensitivity. In the stories in Acts, the new insight or directive from the Holy Spirit, in most instances, took the participants wholly by surprise. (At this distance we can see historical forces at work—in the conferences on Faith and Order we call them "social and cultural factors"—to provide the setting for the new development. But the living Spirit of Christ, not the circumstances, prompted the authentically Christian response.) The church's life in the Spirit, in any case, was a life of joyful spontaneity in obedience to the living Lord. The leading which came to the church did not move counter to reason, did not contradict the gospel; it challenged old prejudices, it counteracted that institutional arthritis which so often stiffens the joints and slows the responses of the body of Christ on earth. It led to continuing reform.

III

The intensive research of our New Testament scholars during the past half century using the methodology known as form-criticism throws a great deal of light on the life of the early church in its response to its living Lord. Like many other new insights deriving from scientific study, form-criticism at first seemed a threat to the securities of Christian faith. I am convinced that now, however, we can draw from its conclusions a fuller understanding than before, not only of the apostolic church, but of the situation of the church in any generation as it seeks to live out its calling in faithful obedience.

According to my amateur understanding, the form-critics are saying something like this: Our synoptic gospels are not formal biographies composed after the methods of modern historical writing, in which a researcher carefully investigates every aspect of his subject, arranges his note-cards in a pattern of careful development, and then synthesizes narrative and exposition in an original literary account. Our gospels are much more like hastily written term papers put together by the scissors-and-paste method; the author simply assembles and imposes some orderly arrangement on a considerable mass of already existing material. If the evangelists had been able to produce their manuscripts on the typewriter and had followed the modern device of single-spacing everything they were quoting from a previous source, their pages would have been mostly solid. And what was all this material which they were quoting? (It is better to say preserving). It was the *preaching* of the apostolic church.

Thus the report of a work of healing or the presentation of a parable with its interpretation is not an objective account written down at the time the incident occurred. It is a distillation of the preaching in the community of faith a generation later. Look carefully at the interpretations of the parables or the brief words of application to life incorporated in the telling of some occurrence in the career of our Lord. These applications are not to problems faced by the disciples in Galilee before the Crucifixion but to issues confronting the church in the second or third or fourth decade of its history. A remembered saying of Jesus arising out of one circumstance provided matter for reflection by the preacher, and the latter's reverent application or conclusion became a word of the Lord in a quite different circumstance. Work through Frederick C. Grant's exegesis of Mark 7:1-23 [3] for example. The account begins with a discussion in Palestine between Jesus and the Pharisees concerning the ritual washing of hands and concludes with the observation, "Thus he declared all foods clean." The problem there introduced was one faced by the Gentile church a generation after the discussion with the Pharisees. Yet can anyone doubt that this was indeed the word of the living Lord to his church? That his spirit was leading his followers out of bondage to ritualism into the mature freedom of men in Christ?

74

Thus far the form-critics take us. Why have we been so slow to discern the theological principle implicit in this historical knowledge? For here we see again the dynamic character of the church's vocation to obedience. We are called as Christians to do the will of God in the *present* moment, in *our* historic situation, even though no decision previously made, no word uttered in the past, speaks precisely to this set of circumstances. In this situation we must look to the leading of the Lord who is the Spirit and must be ready for guidance that takes us on new and uncharted paths. The quality of heroic response to unprecedented demands which was so characteristic of the apostolic church [4] has been too often absent in succeeding generations. When we speak of faithfulness we tend to think of unbudging adherence to old traditions, not glad obedience to the Spirit who would move us out to greater freedom in Christ and an ampler fullness of Christian love. We have far too often failed to remember this in our discussions of the differences among the churches, and so find ourselves deadlocked again and again in the Faith and Order movement. We need to ponder more earnestly the insights which Ernst Käsemann brought as a biblical theologian of the form-critical school to the Fourth World Conference on Faith and Order at Montreal. Is it not true, he asked, "that all tradition and every office of the Church possess authority only so long and in so far as they permit us to perceive the voice of Christ?" [5]

Hans Urs von Balthasar also advances the theological position I am arguing in his recent work on *A Theology of History*.

Man is led into the "deep things of God" in the way described by St. Paul, by being overwhelmed by what has never been seen, heard or felt (1 Cor. ii 9-10), while any knowledge which he thinks he may possess only convicts him of ignorance (1 Cor. viii 2). The Church's knowledge, dogmatic knowledge, is not an exception to this. It is subject to the paradox which applies to all Christian truth, that the content of what is given always overflows to an infinite degree the vessel into which it is poured. The fulfillment given in the New Testament was certainly present, as promise, in the forms of the Old; yet, when it came, everyone who was not prepared to be led on beyond anything he had previously understood, imagined and longed for was scandalized. And by analogy, the believer in the Church must always be ready to make the leap from the old and familiar into the essentially new—the *metanoeite* which lies at the very source of the Gospel—in order to be obedient to the Holy Spirit; leaving the matter of continuity entirely to him, and not turning it into a merely natural category. Not doing theology with the idea that one takes certain given and established premises, and draws some kind of automatic conclusion from them, but taking every step in one's thinking as a direct hearing and obeying of the living Spirit of Jesus Christ.[6]

So the need for reformation continually confronts the church as the demand of the living Christ. In the first three chapters of Revelation the vision of the glorified Lord, followed by the letters to the seven churches of Asia Minor, is a striking example of the call to reform in the New Testament itself. The overwhelming vision of one like a son of man arrayed in glory upon the throne reminds the church of the august transcendence of the victorious Christ. Then in the letters comes a common pattern: (*a*) the encounter of the church with its Lord—"I know your works," (*b*) divine judgment and call for reform—"I have this against you," and (*c*) the promise of renewal—"I will give you."

Whenever the church acknowledges that its Lord deals with it in this way and is prepared to respond in obedience, that church is truly reformed.

IV

At this point I must enter a word of warning concerning a principle set forth in Blake's San Francisco sermon. As one element of its reformed nature, he insisted that the "reunited Church must be truly democratic in its government." My warning is not to Blake, who understands quite well the point I wish to make ("It is the essence of Protestant concern . . . that decisions should generally be made by ordered groups of men under the guidance of the Holy Spirit" [7]), but is directed to American churches generally.

Because our churches observe the *form* of democratic government —indeed the congregational meeting is one of the major sources of our modern democracy—many uninformed persons jump to the conclusion that in a church vote we are seeking to determine the will of the majority. On any question of substance in any church meeting that should never be true. What *most of us want* cannot become—we dare not let it become—the point at issue at all. Rather the question is: What do most of us believe the will of Christ is? We are seeking a common mind as to the next step in our obedience. And we believe that the surest way of determining the leading of the Spirit is for all the people of God to open their minds and hearts in the search for his will. But personal preferences and old prejudices must be rigorously subjugated to our supreme loyalty to Jesus Christ.

Shall we fire the preacher because we don't like what he said on civil rights? If we regard the church as a club where we employ someone to tell us what we like to hear, the answer is yes. (Only we had better stop calling it the church of Christ.) If we believe that the church is the chosen people of God set in the world to do his will and to make it known, then our only question can be, was our minister earnestly trying to declare to us what he believes to be the will of God in the light of the gospel? And if we believe that he was, whether we like it or not is totally immaterial.

As a minister of the word of God I have found myself having to say a great many things I did not like to hear. One of the glories of the faith, symbolized by our great Protestant tradition of the free pulpit, is that as God's people we confess his lordship over all of life and we acknowledge our calling to obedient service. We seek not our own will but his.

V

The biblical view of the church set forth in this chapter is essential to our understanding of God's calling to his people in our times. The doctrine of God's people as summoned in radical obedience to the living Lord frees us both from fear of the unknown and from bad conscience over forsaking peculiarities which were dear to our denominational forefathers but which have no relevance to our mission today. Living under the Holy Spirit, the church is a dynamic community. It is not bound to its own past. Indeed, the only virtue in any historic institution or practice is the degree to which it bears meaningful witness to the gospel.

Christians all over the world believe that in the events of this great ecumenical century the Lord and Head of the church has been trying to break down the walls of separation among his people. We believe that he wills to lead us to a fuller realization of our oneness in him and a manifestation of that oneness to the world. Only as we discern and respond to his divine intention can we hope to receive a church sufficient to these times. "He who has an ear, let him hear what the Spirit says to the churches" (Rev. 3:22). Wherever that happens you will find a church truly reformed. It is servant of the living Lord.

CHAPTER 5
The Church of the Biblical Witness

Any consideration of the church as truly reformed must reckon with the place of Holy Scripture in its life. Protestantism has been classically defined as the religion of the Book. In the words of Chillingworth, "The Bible and the Bible alone is the religion of Protestants." [1]

Because deference to the Scriptures is such a predictable element in any discussion of the Protestant tradition, it was necessary to begin our consideration of a church truly reformed at another point. Every Protestant, and especially the earnest partisan who thrills to the traditional slogans about the Bible, needs to ponder deeply the situation of the apostolic church. It had no corpus of Christian Scripture, but was forced to work out its salvation and to find the shape of its life from the gospel, under the leading of the Spirit. Anyone who believes that the true church can solve its every problem by appealing to some chapter-and-verse requires shock therapy: a realization of the unstructured dynamism of the early Christian community. But the ancient church did produce the New Testament, which believers ever since have held to be inspired by the Holy Spirit and normative for the life of the Christian community. All the great branches of Christendom acknowledge the authority of Scripture.

In this chapter we shall suggest the reformers' intent in exalting the Bible and point out some dangers into which the church has fallen as a result of its misuse. Then we must put ourselves earnestly to the task of reflecting on the rightful place and function of the Scriptures in a church for these times. We shall be led to see, I believe, that a church truly reformed must be a church of the biblical witness.

One of the most dramatic and highly publicized modern observances of Reformation Day was that held in St. Louis in 1945 under the auspices of the Metropolitan Church Federation. Executive secretary of the federation, Clark Walker Cummings and his colleagues worked hard to come up with an appropriate symbol for that occasion. He was elated at their decision. Into the great Kiel Auditorium filed a vast procession of ministers and choirs from many churches. And at the head of the line marched a lad carrying a large open Bible.

The Bible is the obvious symbol of Protestant faith. The heroic statues of Martin Luther present him appealing to the open Book. The witness of traditional reformed church architecture could hardly be more insistent on the point: a plain auditorium barren of symbolic decoration with a lofty center pulpit, surmounted by a massive Bible, for the proclamation of the Word. The Church of Scotland heightens the emphasis with simple dramatic action which introduces the service of worship. A congregational official known as the beadle ascends the high pulpit, opens the Bible, returns to the vestry for the minister, and escorts him to that lofty eminence. From the moment that the minister says, "Let us worship God," it is apparent that he is there to expound the Book. On the American frontier the sign of the Christian faith was not the cross, but the Bible. The celebrated statue of the Pioneer Mother at Ponca City, Oklahoma, represents her as carrying a large volume of Scripture. The circuit rider was known not by a clerical collar but by the Book that he bore. The missionary, here and abroad, was a man with a Bible under his arm. The evangelist preached with an open Bible in one hand. The chief role for earnest laymen and laywomen in the nineteenth century was as teachers in the Bible school. The contemporary revivalist invokes authority for his message with the recurring refrain, "The Bible says. . . !"

There is reason for the symbol. Protestantism has proved itself indeed the religion of the Book. The great reformers found the good news of grace and the assurance of their own justification in reading Galatians and Romans and the Psalms. Their sermons were biblical expositions; their theology was biblical theology, or intended to be. The members of the churches were expected to study the Scripture, to nurture their children on its reading, and to determine the rightness of the preaching by its conformity to the text. Calvin even introduced the biblical languages into his school in Geneva, not for ministers but for laymen. Generations of authors, masters of expression, received their discipline in English style from listening to the words of the King James Bible.

In the American wilderness, leaders of growing religious movements staked everything on the popular knowledge of the New Testament. In my own heritage as a Disciple, for example, there was no written creed, no official statement of theology, no general episcopacy, no ecclesiastical court of orthodoxy. But there was an objective court of appeal: A doctrinal statement was sound if it set forth biblical doctrine. Therefore Christian believers must be men and women of the Book. The great frontier evangelist Walter Scott insisted that any man aspiring to be a deacon (local officer) in the church of Christ should memorize the New Testament: He could surely get a chapter a day by heart, and the whole thing in less than a year. These folk took pride in being known as "walking Bibles."

I

How great the contrast offered by Protestantism today! Except in the receding enclaves of pietism the man with the Bible under his arm is seldom seen. We have officers in our congregations who cannot even find a book in the New Testament if it comes after John. A high school English teacher in a culturally favored community found his pupils guessing that Sodom and Gomorrah were lovers. The old disciplines of regular Bible-reading, in the family or in private, have largely broken down. Students for the ministry appear unfamiliar with the content of Scripture, even by the time they have finished college. The church of this generation has neither taught them the Bible nor motivated them to discover its contents for themselves. In today's church of the Reformation the Bible is a closed book—except perhaps for that unread symbol on the altar. We are the people of the Book we do not read.

There are reasons for this sad condition within modern Protestantism, at least within its liberal and neoorthodox wings.

An old proverb, repudiated by both Jeremiah and Ezekiel, ran:

> The fathers have eaten sour grapes,
> and the children's teeth are set on edge
> (Jer. 31:29; Ezek. 18:2).

We may be permitted a parody, adding another verse to the couplet, to suggest our present situation:

The grandfathers ate the sour grapes,
the teeth of their children were set on edge,
and the children's children get no wine.

To work backward through this triplet, the "children's children"
are the youth of today, largely deprived of meaningful experience
with the Bible because of their fathers' revulsion against the use the
grandfathers made of it. In the reformed (puritan) tradition, within which the great popular churches of nineteenth-century
America stood, the prevailing approach to the Scriptures had become that of legalism. Christians lived by a stern and too often a
loveless discipline, enforced by Bible-quoting elders. Instead of
seeing the sacred volume as a book of life (that is, life here and
now), many had been taught to regard it as a code of law; instead
of the cup of salvation brimming with the wine of the joy that
is in Christ, they knew as religion the unripened grapes of legalism.
The rebellion of their children was a foregone conclusion. Indeed,
the story of American thought and letters through the nineteenth
century is a consistent account of revulsion against puritanical in-
hibition, but the revolt reached its peak in the generation of flaming
youth who drank and squandered their names into headlines—
and a few of them into artistic greatness—in the decade after World
War I. Even within the church, anti-Puritanism and antibiblicism
were dominant moods within the liberal religion of the period. The
Christian rejection of a wrong use of the Bible carried with it a de-
emphasis on the Scripture itself. To keep the children from eating
grapes before they were ripe, the vines were cut off at the ground.
At approximately the same time, traditional assumptions about
the Bible received a succession of rude shocks from the conclusions
of the scientists. "Geology and Genesis" was a perennial topic for
debate, as arguments raged over the age of the earth. Then came
Darwin, and among persons with scientific education the hypothesis

of evolution gained increasing acceptance. Too many ignorant and fearful believers rushed into the fray to "defend the Word of God." While religious liberals tried to work out an understanding of the Christian faith in harmony with the knowledge discovered by modern science, fundamentalists insisted on the inerrancy of the Scriptures and quoted the Bible against their liberal brethren. Such obscurantism served only to drive to greater extremes of reaction those Christians who were already in rebellion against the old legalism.

The revulsion of the sophisticated liberal or neoorthodox minister against fundamentalist legalism and literalism often inflicted a permanent trauma; such a man became so fearful of the appearance of fundamentalism that instead of being antibiblicist his ministry risked being nonbiblical. He so vigorously rejected the old theories of mechanical inspiration that he tended to be afraid of pointing his people to the Word of God made known in the Scriptures. He reacted so violently when a popular evangelist declared, "The Bible says!" that he virtually left the Bible a closed book to his congregation. Perhaps I exaggerate. But do I?

Quite aside from the bitter controversies over the Bible and their unfortunate aftermath, other difficulties confront the church. Increasingly the antiquity of scriptural thought-forms presents a problem in comprehension to the contemporary, secular, positivistic mind; it is not enough to move from the archaic diction of the King James to the clarity of the Revised Standard Version or the pointed paraphrase of J. B. Phillips. The categories of thought are strange: sin, sacrifice, atonement, demons, miracles, heaven, hell, judgment, righteousness, grace. Much of the language used *about* the Bible carries traditional connotations embarrassing to the sophisticated minister: inspiration, revelation, Word of God. Perhaps he has worked out a personally satisfying reformulation of such terms, but he suspects hypocrisy in other men's use of them and sometimes fears it in his own.

Beyond all this has been the shattering effect of the critical studies of recent decades. The presuppositions which made the Bible the dynamic authority of the Protestant Reformation have, it would seem, been swept away by the scholars. Most ministers, it is to be hoped, have struggled through to a meaningful position, but the issues are so complex and the traditional assumptions so intertwined with popular emotion that many have hesitated to face them with the churches, or even with selected members. Yet the failure of the teachers to deal with the problem has not saved the people from confusion.

The old sense of transcendence, of a Word from on high, has gradually dissipated. Laymen are hardly prepared to deny the authority of the Bible; they might even be shocked at such a denial, but it holds little meaning in their lives. As a seminary professor in the biblical field remarked to me, concerning his students: "They don't really believe it's the Word of God any more. So they don't read it." Abraham Joshua Heschel graphically analyses our problem: "The sense of the mystery and *transcendence* of what is at stake in the Bible is lost in the process of analysis. As a result, we have brought about the desanctification of the Bible." [2]

Obviously we have been describing a disease of the contemporary church and not a state of health. To change the figure, it is an exaggerated case of adolescent rebellion: A youngster resents his parents, however admirable, for belonging to an older generation. But this very rebelliousness, this resentment, is in itself a sign that the adolescent is still immature. Granted that mechanical proof-texting, uncharitable heresy-hunting, and unprofitable debating became for a time too characteristic of our spiritual forebears. Granted that youngsters and oldsters rattled off memory verses learned by rote with little attendant grace of life. Granted that some of them tried to imprison the Holy Spirit in an ancient form of words. Grant all the other limitations of the old legalistic biblicism. These are not weaknesses of our churches today. To think of them as posing a threat would be laughable if the situation were not so pathetic. Is it not time that we outgrow our adolescent rebellion, work out a mature concept of the Bible to replace the childish notions we must put away, and ascribe to the Scriptures their rightful place in the life of the church?

In the case of every one of us, our indebtedness to the Bible is immeasurable, and if this is true of us as individual Christians, it is infinitely more true of the church as community of believers. The very language of our faith, its thought-forms, its style, its ethical presuppositions, its habitual patterns of devotion, we owe to the Bible. And our self-conscious rebellion has not taken us so far away from the vast authority it exercises over our lives as we are prone to imagine.

A church truly reformed is the church of the biblical witness. Historically we know that to be true. Existentially we must also confess it to be true. If the church is to find her true calling in obedience to God she must listen to the word that he speaks through the holy Scriptures and restore them to a meaningful place— a place assigned by honest reason, not mere sentimental tradition— within the life of the believing community. Such a development is in fact now going on in many parts of Christendom.

II

How then may modern Christians think of the Bible? From our stance as men of the twentieth century and men of faith in Jesus Christ, how are we honestly to speak of the Scriptures and their function in our common life? I make five brief suggestions.

A. *The Bible is the church's record coming down from those men of faith who participated in the saving events recounted in the gospel of Christ* (and, before him, in the story of Israel).

For all we know and have known for nearly two thousand years, the Scriptures are our sole witness to the great Event which constitutes the historic origin of our faith. A few phrases about Israel, to be sure, and a fragmentary word about Jesus of Nazareth appear here and there in the secular records of antiquity, but nothing to give us a true picture of Israel's trust in God, of the ministry and teaching of Jesus, of the life of the early church. Imagine for a moment that the books of the New Testament had never been collected together and so had been lost to history. Think then of the excitement that would sweep the Christian world if in some cave by the Dead Sea only one of these writings were to be found! With what eagerness we should read: "The beginning of the gospel of Jesus Christ . . ." (Mark 1:1). Or "It seemed good to me . . . to write an orderly account for you, most excellent Theophilus, that you may know the truth concerning the things of which you have been informed" (Luke 1:3-4). Or "Now I would remind you, brethren, in what terms I preached to you the gospel, which you received, in which you stand, by which you are saved" (I Cor. 15:1-2).

Imagine the care with which the manuscript would be guarded (even if a late copy of the original), the eagerness to procure copies and translations, the fondness with which they would be read, the spiritual revival that would engulf Christendom! Yet all these books now are ours, our record of the deeds that changed the world.

(It is worthy of note that the canonical record has imposed effective limitations on the growth of speculation and legend. One historian dryly observed concerning the riot of incredible tales about the Virgin Mary which grew up in the virtual vacuum left by the Gospels: "If the early Christians had known more about the Mother of the Lord, the medieval mind would have known far less." [3] We do know enough about the Lord himself, thanks to the testimony of the Gospels.)

B. *The Bible is the witness of the earliest believers to the meaning of the events into which they had entered.* It is the abiding testimony of the early church's faith.

For my own part I believe that the insights of the New Testament writers into the meaning of those things which had happened among them were inspired of the Holy Spirit, that their profound understanding of the Cross and the Resurrection was a divine gift, that the illumination of the Spirit effected the qualitative difference which Christians discern between these writings, taken as a whole, and any other literature which anyone should undertake to place alongside them.

Some of us, I suppose, would not miss the book of Numbers greatly or the Letter of Jude. But as a composite work the Bible is unique. Through it the men most deeply involved in the reception of the gospel speak to us of its meaning.

That which was from the beginning, which we have heard, which we have seen with our eyes, which we have looked upon and touched with our hands, concerning the word of life . . . we proclaim also to you, so that you may have fellowship with us; and our fellowship is with the Father and with his Son Jesus Christ (1 John 1:1-3).

Whatever this man's cultural circumstances, however deficient his knowledge concerning the age of the earth or the movements of the solar system, whoever indeed he may have been, he speaks out of the believing community who had discerned the meaning of God's deed in Jesus Christ. And this ancient word falls on our ears also as good news.

C. *The Bible is the church's primary means of handing on its tradition as an objective body of data remembered and understood.*

In a sense this point is an elaboration of points A and B; yet it calls attention to an important function of the Bible within the church.

We should doubtless know something of the ministry of our Lord and the mystery of the church's life, had the New Testament never been written and the entire burden of traditioning been left to the preachers and the teachers. But imagine the confusion. We all can recall arguments we have heard about the details of some biblical statement and the ease with which these have been settled by looking up the passage in question. Think of the chaos if there had been nothing to look up—only conflicting memories of something heard long ago. Without the Bible, a good deal of stabilization might have been possible through the eucharistic liturgy; we should know at least the major elements of the gospel. But so much is omitted there, except as provided from the New Testament lections—the Sermon on the Mount, the parables, the Johannine discourses, virtually the entire book of Acts and the Epistles. How terribly deprived our corporate spiritual life would be without Rom. 8, Rom. 12, I Cor. 13, II Cor. 4, Col. 1, and the Letter to the Ephesians, to select only a few passages!

Think of the vocabulary of faith which is common to biblically literate Christians and of the pathetic impoverishment of our Christian discourse, especially the language of prayer, without the common heritage of the two Testaments.

D. *The Bible is a source of continuing illumination to those who read it and hear it in faith,* particularly to the church, that community which regularly exposes her life to the witness of the Scripture and ponders the meaning of that witness.

In this way the Bible comes to exert a far more profound type of authority than that conceived in the old fundamentalism: "If it's written in the Bible, it's so." How many honest and sensitive minds have resisted the pressure imposed by such a conception, pressure to believe the incredible, the unreasonable, the unworthy. Fortunately we are no longer bound by such notions. But to those who live familiarly with the Bible, who take the trouble to understand its categories of thought, new light is repeatedly breaking forth from the sacred page. The value in any work of literature is that if I really come to understand one other person, I know something more about myself. Through pondering the Bible we know afresh that company of believers who first participated in the work of Christ and thus we know our own situation far more clearly. Increasingly those of us who seek in reverence to discern the will of God find in the Bible an authority which is not confining but liberating, not darkening but enlightening the mind.

E. *Thus the Bible becomes the primary instrument of the Holy Spirit in the guidance of the church.*

This witness to the central event of our salvation and the meaning of the event for our human condition was, we believe, inspired by the Spirit; which is to say that only men who had come into a transforming relationship with the risen Christ could have written these books. And in the reading of them now we who are the church find ourselves once again brought into such confrontation with our living Lord. The reading too often becomes cold and mechanical, but when we attend with an eager heart, it is not so. The witness of the Spirit, to use Calvin's term, confirms and energizes the witness of the written word; then as Christians we discover ourselves no longer reading of events long ago, but entering into actual experience of the good news.

> But warm, sweet, tender, even yet
> A present help is He;
> And faith has still its Olivet,
> And love its Galilee.[4]

The reading of the Scripture becomes, in effect, a sacrament. Through this testimony the good news of God is made a contemporary reality in the life of the church. It is this reality to which we Christians refer when we say that the Word of God comes to us through the Bible.

III

On reflection, it is obvious why a church truly reformed must be a church of the biblical witness. Since God in his gracious providence has caused the holy Scriptures to be written for our learning, the church which slights them, ignores them, or fails to expose her life to their witness does so at her own peril. That being true, we may properly ask, How does the church accord to the Bible a worthy place in her corporate life?

Here are four suggestions concerning the place which rightly belongs to the Scriptures in a church for these times:

A. *The Bible holds a determinative place in the liturgy of the church.*

The readings from the Scriptures are properly elevated as great moments in the worship of God's people. What irony there is in the trivialization of the reading which has overtaken so many "free churches" of the Protestant tradition! I have been in Sunday morning worship in which the entire Scripture selection consisted of three verses from the gospel. I have heard a minister apologize for having been asked to read "an *entire chapter*" of the New Testament in a church convention. In some congregations there is no passage read out from pulpit or lectern, except the alternate sentences in the responsive reading "from the back of the hymnal." Despite such horrible examples, my impression is that a proper respect for the reading of the Scripture in worship is on the increase. More careful attention is being given to the choice of passages for public reading. Ministers in the "free churches" are increasing their use of a lectionary, or schedule of selections designed both to cover the sweep of the biblical message and to accord with the seasons of the church year. There is some evidence of recovery from the mania for haste and of a return to the use of both Old Testament and New Testament selections in each service. Something is to be said for the practice in the reformed churches of reading in succession a passage from the Old Testament, one from the gospels, and one from the epistles, all bearing on a common theme.

Throughout the order of worship, the established liturgies (Orthodox, Roman, Lutheran, Episcopal) make large use of biblical selections, particularly from the Psalms and from the hymns of the early church. In its typically austere way, the early worship of the reformed churches also relied heavily on biblical phrases. Who can forget the sense of majesty that brooded over the worship of a humble Scottish or Welsh or Swiss congregation, where the minister seldom used a word of his own except in prayer or sermon, and his language even then was burdened with biblical phrases? Under the limited circumstances of life on the frontier, and especially under the impact of revivalism, worship in the American free churches fell into an easy, sometimes shabby informality. The design was to get people to "enjoy" the service, especially the "gospel songs," and to respond to the personality of the preacher. The cost was heavy. The stately biddings to prayer, to offering, even to the Lord's table in the language of Scripture gave way to a chatty didacticism and moralizing on the part of the minister, with a too frequent attempt at "inspiration" by a "little bit of poetry." Free worship lost the air of mystery which had characterized it in its noble simplicity. One of the ironies of history is the fading use of Scripture in the services of many Protestant churches, whereas the Roman mass continues to be freighted with an abundance of biblical passages.

Under the influence of the liturgical movement, a more thoughtful understanding of worship is growing throughout Christendom.

In the churches with established orders, the tendency is toward simplicity, toward stripping away meaningless motion or quaint tradition. In the free churches there is a growing sense of dignity and of the importance of involving the people with the minister in responses and prayers, so that the action truly involves the total priesthood of believers. Much work needs to be done in instructing church members concerning the meaning of corporate praise. Among other things, the importance of using the Bible in worship needs to be more fully understood.

B. *The Bible is the inspiration of the church's preaching; it provides the essential content of the message and the forms in which it is memorably conveyed.* Preaching is the church's proclamation of the good news of what God has done in Christ. Hence true preaching is biblical preaching. Such proclamation characterizes the essence of a church truly reformed. Indeed, it is impossible to think of the authentic work of preaching apart from an intimate involvement with the Scripture. The importance of this relationship is being rediscovered today.

At the beginning, a proper Protestant sermon was the exposition of a particular passage of Scripture, usually a lengthy paragraph if not a chapter. Hence it was both proclamatory and didactic, its purpose being to establish the people in sound doctrine. In time, popular preachers reduced the basis of the sermon to a text of a verse or two; it was more manageable in length. Some were adept at portraying the great characters of the Bible. While some great textual preachers consistently proclaimed the gospel to the life of their day, it must be admitted that too much preaching, anchored in the past, degenerated into disquisition on ancient history or the ideas and problems of antiquity. The popular topical preachers of the nineteenth century and the "life-centered" preachers of the twentieth worked hard to make the Bible contemporary once more. But with the uncertainty about the Bible which characterized the times, their sermons easily degenerated into lectures on current issues or "inspirational talks" with little scriptural content, even by implication.

The time is ripe for a revival of biblical preaching keyed to the needs and moods of our contemporaries. Laymen brought up in relative ignorance are showing an eager interest in the great themes of the Scripture, as these speak to our deepest spiritual needs. Much is being said about the "sacramental" character of preaching. In the proclamation of the acts of God in Christ, the grace he then revealed is actualized, made present to the hearts of the hearers.

C. *The Bible is the basic resource for the education of the people in the disciplines of discipleship.*

The whole understanding of the church as "truly reformed" demands a comprehending and committed membership. Historically the Reformation followed hard upon the expansion of popular education associated with the Renaissance, and the invention of printing with movable type. The reformers appealed to a literate laity and did everything within their power to spread the teaching of the Christian faith. Their understanding of the church as a corporate priesthood of believers required that the entire membership "grow in the grace and knowledge of our Lord and Savior Jesus Christ " (II Pet. 3:18). The Bible was central in the work of teaching; one of the chief concerns of the reformers was to translate it into the various languages of the people of Europe.

This is not the place for a survey of Christian education across the past several centuries, for an analysis of recent shortcomings, or for the sketching of a theory of religious pedagogy. Suffice it to say that the knowledge of the Bible and the ability to use it on the part of adults are in a woeful state in our American churches. Doubtless the chief cause is the pattern of the adult Sunday school class which still prevails in most churches: the "Uniform Lesson" is "taught" in large classes which meet primarily for fellowship, inspiration, and perhaps the confirmation of prejudice, but not for education in any commonly accepted meaning of the word. The teacher is really a lay exhorter. He seldom uses so simple a pedagogical device as blackboard and chalk. The class members almost never study before coming; they do not bring notebooks or pencils to take anything down. No one expects to learn anything! Rarely are copies of the Bible used by anyone, except possibly the teachers.

The paragraph above is not intended as diatribe but as description. It does not imply that nothing is appropriate for adult study in the churches except the Bible. The outrage arises from the fact that no teaching of the Bible is going on in the vast enterprise of the so-called "Bible classes." Protestantism stands naked to its foes— to the world, the flesh, the devil, and (for the sophisticated) Zen— when its laity are ignorant of the Word.

The time has come for serious study on the part of Christian adults in the American churches. This means enlisting groups of persons who intend to learn something, who will undertake study outside the brief class session, who will keep notes, who will review, who will learn the joy of progress in understanding and in the mastery of material. Certainly many of the elective units now available on current problems of individuals and of society, on Christian doctrine, on "churchmanship" are valid and important. But nothing is more crucial to the whole enterprise than teaching Christians the effective use of the Bible. In some groups this means beginning at the childish level of learning to recite the books of the Old and New Testaments in order and practice in looking up passages. It means a rapid survey of the major portions of the Scriptures and of the landmarks in the unfolding of biblical history. It means telling the story of translation and some introduction to the various renderings which are available. It means intensive study of particular books of the Bible, with all the members of the class holding their own copies, following along in the text, taking their turn at reading, and being persuaded to ask any question, however elementary or shocking it may seem. When a group has been exposed to this kind of procedure for some months, it is then ready for topical courses, which use the Bible as a "resource," and for the more sophisticated procedures of "Bible study in depth" which are now gaining acceptance.

All Christians need to develop the disciplines of daily Bible reading and prayer, in families or in private. However remote the kings of Israel may seem, however difficult some passages in the prophets, every Christian can profit from daily reading in the Psalter and in the Gospels. The old rule of "a chapter a day" was perhaps perfunctory and unimaginative, and motivation often played out on the dreary wastes of the wilderness of Sinai somewhere in Leviticus. But there is no substitute for a regular pattern of reading if men and women are to keep fresh in their knowledge of the Scripture and if it is to provide spiritual illuminaton for their daily walk.

D. *The Bible stands in constant judgment over the church.*

In truth, God is the judge. But the Bible provides that authentic witness to the gospel by which the church must constantly measure her proclamation, her life, and her every activity.

We have by now gained sufficient maturity in our attitude toward the Bible that it is evident we are not insisting on a "proof text" for everything in the life of the church. The Scriptures are not a compilation of divine legislation. But they are accepted throughout the church as setting forth all that is essential to man's salvation, as presenting the early church's understanding of the will of God for all mankind. Obviously the Bible does not present specific plans to be followed in the cold war. It does not offer ready solutions to many of the practical problems that will arise in the Consultation on Church Union as it works toward a specific plan for the reunion

96

of Christ's church. But the Bible does keep our attention on those realities which are central to Christian faith and life. When the church wanders off toward humanism, or rationalism, or legalism, or introversion, or slackness of discipline, or conformity to the culture, or coldness of heart, the Bible is the corrective to turn it back to the path of life. This is why a church sufficient to these times, or to any times that we can imagine will keep the Scriptures at the center of its life.

IV

A church truly reformed is the church of the biblical witness. The growing interest in Bible study throughout worldwide Christendom is one of the surest harbingers of continuing reformation in our day. Nowhere is this more evident than at the point of ecclesiology. Throughout Christendom—Protestant, Orthodox, Roman Catholic, East and West, "older" and "younger"—a common mind is emerging concerning the church as the reconciled people of God. This is the visible community in which God wills to make manifest to the world his purpose of uniting all things in Christ. Thus the ecumenical movement is becoming ever more and more self-consciously a movement inspired by the biblical witness.

Within such a context it is apparent that many of our old denominational distinctions must go. We used to justify them by proof texts. Champions of rival Protestant sects armed themselves with scriptural quotations to clash in debate over the truth of their competing positions. Earnest Christians sternly appealed to chapter-and-verse to justify their lack of fellowship with others who named the name of Christ but whose beliefs or practices, they felt, were erroneous. Denominational preaching was expected to be polemical. The story is told of the old Kentuckian who reprimanded the sectarianism of the Christians with a whimsical parody of I John

3:14; "We know we have passed out of death into life because we *fight* the brethren." [5]

Out of such pathetic partiality and spiritual blindness the good Spirit of God is now leading his people as they come to a fuller understanding of the divine purpose through the common study of holy Scripture. We do not find therein a detailed pattern for the church as institution, nor specific heavenly directions for practical means of overcoming our denominational divisions. But the will of God for his people to be the community of the reconciled is clear. The essence of what it means for the church to be truly evangelical, truly reformed, and truly catholic is a vision which he gives to us through the pages of the Bible.

CHAPTER 6
The Need for Recurring Reformation

Living under the mandate of the divine Word, the church is constantly placed under judgment and called to renewed obedience. Even the earliest community of Christians, as we have seen, was repeatedly confronted by its living Lord with the demand for change. Indeed, the typical action of the Holy Spirit in dealing with the apostolic church was to confront it with the necessity of being made over.

I

Through the long centuries since the days of its beginnings, the story of the church's spiritual renewal has been the story of repeated reformation. Sometimes this meant returning to an earlier doctrine or practice from which God's people had fallen away in ignorance or sloth; but not always so. As often as not the reforma-

99

tion involved the introduction of a new emphasis, or of an old emphasis in a new expression. The whole history of the church documents this affirmation; all that can be done here is to suggest some major topics for an outline.

When the Roman emperors ceased their persecutions and the church was growing comfortable and soft, uneasy Christians remembered the blood of the martyrs. Heroes were needed in a new mold—laymen called to lives of discipline and self-denial. Basil, bishop of Caesarea, and Benedict of Nursia wrote their monastic rules, providing in communities of prayer and labor powerful instruments of continuing reform.

When the imperial legions fell back from northern and western Europe before the blond savages from the forests of Scandinavia, the Irish monks called the church out of its cowering introversion. In its original missionary sense, an apostolic succession of intrepid evangelists—Columba, Columban, Willibrord, Boniface—carried the gospel from Ireland to Scotland to England to France to the Low Countries to Germany to Switzerland to Italy.

When the Western church of the tenth and eleventh centuries fell into moral decay, the great reform movement arose. The Emperor Henry II, Pope Leo IX, Peter Damian, Cardinal Humbert, and Pope Gregory VII gave themselves in efforts to revivify monastic zeal, to cleanse the clergy of moral corruption, and finally to free the papacy from the power of the secular governments.

When the church of the thirteenth century had grown fat and proud once more, Francis of Assisi and the Order of the Little Brothers set an example of apostolic poverty and sought to call the Christian community back to a sense of mission and service.

When the Roman See had become the plaything and the prize of rival political powers in Renaissance Italy, the conciliar movement sought reform through efforts to restrict papal autocracy and to

31663

submit major issues to the judgment of councils representing the whole church.

When the cynical exploitation of popular credulity and late medieval superstition had grown to scandalous proportions, such Renaissance humanists as Sir Thomas More, John Colet, and Erasmus of Rotterdam strove through consecrated scholarship to free the church of ignorance.

When the church had become cluttered with traditions and practices which denied or obscured the gospel the great Protestant reformers placed the good news of God's justifying grace back at the center of her life.

When the membership of the Christian body had become indistinguishable from the population of the state and many persons "born into" the church had no sense of personal commitment, Anabaptists and other sectarians contended for the freedom of the church from the state and for adult conversion to Christ as Lord.

When the old church was still preoccupied with its internal concerns and with the threat of Protestantism, Ignatius Loyola founded the Society of Jesus to bear the Christian message to the new centers of power in the emergent social order—the national courts, secondary education, and the vast new worlds opened by the explorers and *conquistadores*. (In Rome stands a great church, the Gesù, its ceiling covered with a painting of the Seven Seas and the Five Continents to which the Jesuits carried the gospel as Europe awoke from provincialism.)

When the concerns of seventeenth century Protestantism had become fixed on trivialities of doctrinal controversy which was often irrelevant and sometimes ugly, the Pietists called Christians once more to a distinctive way of life, to spiritual discipline, and to mission.

When the Church of England had fallen into a cold formalism

that brought no meaningful witness to the victims of the Industrial Revolution, the eighteenth-century Evangelicals (especially the Wesleys) sought to awaken the church to new life, to confront sinful men with the transforming power of the gospel, and to overcome the evils of a dissolute and brutalized society.

When American Christians had centered their attention on the personal satisfactions of religion and on advancing their particular denominations, humanitarians and Social Gospelers undertook to turn them from lives of spiritual self-indulgence and to confront the world with the demands of the kingdom of God.

When Christians of our own century remained divided by old hostilities and aloof from one another, the ecumenical reformation arose to call us out of our separation into a realization of our oneness in Christ.

Each of these reforms, we believe, has been a gift of God to the church through the Holy Spirit. In every case, the fires of reform began to glow as some particular emphasis within the Scriptures took on an incandescent relevance to the needs of the time. Consider the impact with which our Lord's strongest words about self-denial spoke to the monks and the friars; the power with which the letters to the Romans and Galatians brought the grace of God to men of the sixteenth century distraught by anxiety over their sin and by the fear of death; or the peculiar force with which the Epistle to the Ephesians speaks in a world divided between East and West, between black and white, and to a church which God is calling to unity. So the Spirit works through the Scripture.

Historically there have been four areas of major emphasis for reformers. The first is life and morals, the second is doctrine, the third is institution, and the fourth is mission. Whenever the gospel is denied or obscured at any of these points, the church is due for reform. Whenever she grows negligent in her calling, it is time that, in the Spirit, she should hear her Lord say, "I have this against you." And whenever she responds in penitent obedience she receives the renewing gift of life in the Spirit.

What is the Holy Spirit saying to the churches we know? At what particular points is it necessary for the churches to submit themselves to the judgment of God if they are to be truly reformed? I briefly suggest four areas where I believe the Spirit is taking issue with us.

II

The first is in the realm of life and morals: It is the cold propriety of our religion.

No one can deny that the church occupies a sizeable place in contemporary American life. Two thirds of the population in our free society claim some religious affiliation. Contributions to religious organizations exceeded two billion dollars last year. Magnificent new buildings for congregations, church colleges, benevolent homes, hospitals, and ecclesiastical bureaucracies are rising all over the country. Furthermore the Christian faith has far more meaning to a large part of our population, particularly at times of testing, than the cynical observer may have imagined. In occasions of national or community crisis, our people turn instinctively to the churches. There remains a strong tendency—perhaps it is even growing—to present the symbols of religion at public events. All these manifestations I have mentioned are indications that Christianity is firmly established in the life of our people.

But that is just the cause for concern: This has too many features of a religious establishment, a social heirloom, a function of the culture. For the most part it is characterized by a routine propriety, a coolness of spirit that worships in air-conditioned comfort and seldom exercises itself to the warmth of perspiration. Every pastor knows a host of good Christians, but aside from the crackpots, how many are excited about their faith? In the sophisticated

103

mood of our times we are not quite sure that it is good form to manifest religious emotion; on occasion we permit gentle laughter in church, but weeping might be considered in poor taste. And above all things we must be proper.

A church truly reformed is a church excited about the will of God. Certainly the apostolic church, which was so profoundly marked by the power of the Holy Spirit, manifested an intensity in her preaching and worship and response which are customarily lacking among us. The great eras of reformation have come when men were "aglow with the Spirit" (Rom. 12:11). It is significant that two such rational and respected churchmen as Lesslie Newbigin and Henry Pitney Van Dusen have pointed out our need within the ecumenical movement for the witness of the Pentecostal churches.

I am not proposing that we expend our efforts in whipping up emotional froth. Something in me deeply resented the autocratic manipulations of the old-time revival song leader with all his gimmicks to get me where he wanted me. The pomposity of old-fashioned oratory with its pathos, its quavering, and its prancing, is properly dismissed by our generation as "ham." Nor am I suggesting that we become frantic in an effort to bring on spiritual renewal. The power of the Holy Spirit is a gift we can neither drum up nor "structure in." But it is a blessing which God constantly offers his church, and which we dare not refuse or ignore.

I am proposing that we heed the apostolic admonition: "Do not quench the Spirit" (I Thess. 5:19). In the preaching of the gospel, in worship which regularly brings us to the Lord's table, in the work and fellowship of the church, in the study of our faith, in evangelism, in Christian witness to our society, in any one of these separately, and certainly in all of them together, God has provided sufficient channels for spiritual renewal—if only we are open to the possibility and sensitive in our response. What a difference it would make if some Sunday a congregation should come to church saying, "This time it's for real." What a difference it does make when a minister enters the chancel or pulpit expecting something to happen. The great reformations, their leaders would have said, were gifts from God, but how eager the reformers were to be used, how earnest and responsive! A church truly reformed constantly exposes her life in expectation to the renewing Spirit of God.

III

In the realm of doctrine, reform is constantly necessary and constantly recurring. The minds of men are restless and active, continually being confronted by the questions of life and destiny, continually seeking new answers, or at least reexamining and reshaping the old ones. All this is to be expected, for every generation stands where no man has stood before. The human situation, as described in Chap. 2, is pretty much the same throughout the long career of mankind. But the particular historical circumstances, the knowledge of the world, the data available for reflection and explanation, the mood of the times—all these vary with every passing decade. So theology, which is faith seeking understanding, is fluid, even though the human situation and the facts of the gospel remain unchanged.

In seeking understanding, the faith of any generation must think in the thought-forms of the times, must wrestle with the questions implicit in the peculiar history of those times. Thus any given theological formulation becomes both relevant to its own times and bound by their particular limitations. It may make use of fresh insights into the biblical witness which its unique perspective has made possible. Yet concurrently it will doubtless be blind to or unmoved by some other emphasis of the Scriptures which may speak with great power to an earlier or a later generation.

It will not solve the problem simply to admonish the theologian, "Just stick to the Bible." That misses the whole point. If we could

105

be content just to read the Bible and ask no questions (and if such a servile attitude were proper for Christians), the theological task would be unnecessary. Precisely because our minds must interact with the biblical witness, all Christians are inevitably theologians of a sort.

On the other hand, if each generation of believers were merely to reexamine its inherited formulations in the light of new historical conditions and to propose a "restatement" more in keeping with the new mind of the times, theology would be merely fluid. There would be no necessary reformation of doctrine. Indeed, each successive adaptation, in the nature of the case, would be farther and farther from historic Christian belief as previously understood. By such a process such a bizarre emergent as Islam actually did come forth. Unquestionably the novel emphases of his preaching seemed to the prophet Mohammed to be more relevant to the needs of his desert contemporaries than did the prevailing forms of Christianity as he understood them. (As "objective" observers in the twentieth century we might well be inclined to agree.) Other similar examples might be adduced. The history of Unitarianism is in one respect a more instructive instance of the process of mere fluidity than is that of Islam. For the teachings of Mohammed were absolutized by his followers, whereas the way of Unitarianism remained a "quest." Outside those conservative circles which are content with tradition, therefore, contemporary Unitarian thought is scarcely recognizable as in any sense determined by Christian norms. The present mood of this faith is strikingly different from that of early nineteenth-century Unitarianism in America, which began as an almost evangelical form of the Christian message, its peculiar protest being directed primarily against the harsher doctrines of Calvinism.

How then does the church assure a continual reform of theology which will hold constantly to the Christian center? How avoid that mere fluidity which dissolves into formlessness and trickles away into nothing? To a church truly reformed the answer is clear. It involves the role of the Bible. For each generation of Christians must do more than merely reexamine inherited formulations in the light of new historical conditions and propose restatements more in keeping with the mind of the times. Rather we reexamine our inherited formulations once more *in the light of the biblical witness,* indeed in the light of our new perspective on the biblical witness which was not possible to the generation before us. Not only that. When we have worked out our "reformulation" as moderns, we must put to it the questions which the Bible asks. Theology is, in effect, a continuing dialogue between the Scriptures and the contemporary faith. This repeated questioning of our own assumptions by the Bible is the essential element in the continuing reform of doctrine. The current of Christian thought oscillates across a field defined by the two poles: the biblical witness and the contemporary mind. Either pole left by itself is lifeless. When the two are brought close enough together to establish a field, the spark jumps between them and light and power are evident.

A crucial question then to be asked by each new generation of Christians is not merely, "What do we think of the faith of our fathers?" Equally important are the questions: "What can we hear the Bible saying to the faith of our fathers?" "What then do we say to that?" "What now do we hear the Bible saying to what we have said?" By submitting consciously to this continuing dialogue we are spared the dangers both of biblicism and of conformity to ideological fads.

Consider the exciting dialogue between the Bible and the modern mind which went on in the creative days of American liberal theology. Here was a generation of Christian thinkers ready at last to come to terms with the world view of modern science. The positive accomplishment of these earnest men represents an achievement on which it is inconceivable that the church should ever turn its back. No responsible Christian will henceforth try to maintain, for example, that the book of Genesis provides scientific knowledge concerning the physical processes of the earth's formation. The liberals pointed the way toward a rugged honesty on the part of the Christian faith as it deals with secular knowledge, toward an understanding of the gospel completely unafraid of modern science. For this we must be profoundly grateful.

Nevertheless, as believers of a later generation we can see that the eyes of many liberals were dazzled by romantic hopes concerning the promise of science. With many other men of their time, they extended the evolutionary hypothesis from the biological to the historical realm and thus espoused the unrealistic notion of inevitable progress. This led them to pin their hopes on an assumed upward movement of human history toward the fulfillment of the kingdom of God. Thus they were blinded to the persistent reality of sin, both in the social order and in the lives of individual men and women. The Bolshevik terror in Russia, the atrocities of Nazism in Germany, the terrible ordeal of two World Wars therefore came as a cruel shock to these high-minded men. Indeed, Reinhold Niebuhr maintained that they were unable to provide responsible moral guidance to mankind in a critical era because they had dismissed too lightly from their thinking the biblical doctrine of evil.

So our present generation of theologians has radically revised the liberal pattern of thought with respect to human nature and society while gratefully retaining the liberal accommodation with science. Biblical concepts of sin, judgment, and grace have provided much food for contemporary thought, as have also biblical insights into creation, history, and consummation. Thus an important reformation of doctrine has taken place.

In all honesty we must admit however that it was not the Bible alone, but the turn of events in the twentieth century, which led our contemporary theologians to submit the notions of human goodness and of inevitable progress to such searching examination. This is indeed as it should be. The prophets understood long ago that God speaks to his people through contemporary events. For the Christian pondering the meaning of the perplexing experiences through which he has lived, the Bible provides insight which enables him to discern something of what God is saying in these dread circumstances.

Since many thoughtful men, and not Christians alone, have been troubled by the unhappy events of our times, the stylish optimism of the nineteenth century has given way to a darker intellectual mood known as existentialism. Scores of talented novelists, dramatists, poets, painters, and philosophers have come forth with an approach to life which longs for the fulfillment of its promises but cries out in indignation that these promises must always be shattered on the jagged rocks of meaninglessness, suffering, and death. Many Christians seeking a critique of the bland optimism of the liberals were naturally attracted to the insights of their own contemporaries among the existentialists concerning the human situation. There is no need to illustrate. In the sermons of the sophisticated the names Sartre, Kafka, Camus, Heidegger, run like a monotonous litany.

My point is that much which passes for sophisticated contemporary theology, while fully cognizant of the biblical view of man's sin, takes insufficient account of the biblical joy in redemption. Indeed the great contrast between so much current Christian writing and the pages of the New Testament is precisely at this point. The Bible is aglow with gladness. No matter how darkly the apostles painted the human situation, they always countered with the good news of God's gift of life and cleansing in Jesus Christ. Contemporary theology, then, has done a good job in submitting the liberal formulation to the searching of the biblical point of view.

What needs to be done now is to submit the existentialist formulation of the Christian faith to a similar searching.

In such a manner the reformation of theology goes on. In the dialogue between the Bible and the modern mind, the church continues as a living community of redemption, sustained and illuminated by the Holy Spirit of God.

IV

A third area of current reform to which I would direct attention is institutional: It is the structure of denominationalism.

With American Protestants scattered among 222 denominations, even though ninety percent of them belong to twenty-two major families, our Christian fellowship and witness are ridiculously fractured. For all our cooperation in councils of churches and the contemporary spirit of good will (which is understood as never registering public disapproval of another man's religion), we cannot pretend that this fragmentation does not weaken the Christian cause or that the reasons for it are significant. When one reflects on the daily work of an American Protestant minister, whether in village or city, and how everything he does is complicated, made difficult, compromised, or vitiated by the denominational system, our patience with it becomes unforgivable. Sometimes we rationalize it with the plea that the competition keeps the church on her toes. Such competition bleeds the church white. Oliver C. Schroeder of the Law School at Western Reserve University can set us right on this point. The church's competition, he observed in a recent discussion, is with evil, with poverty, with segregation, with irreligion. By no canon in the Christian scheme are Episcopalians, Disciples, or Pentecostals rightly in competition with Methodists, Presbyterians, or Baptists. Our relationships with any of these brethren, with Eastern Orthodox, with Roman Catholics, with anyone who names the name of Christ are to be seen in a totally different way. Competition has been forced on us by our acquiescence in denomination-al multiplicity.

Furthermore, denominationalism is an anachronism. The dis-agreements that divided our great-great-grandfathers—and the origin of most denominations goes back farther than that—are no longer adequate reasons for our separation as Christians. Our church members know this. In many American congregations now, *most* of the members come from denominations other than that with which they are presently affiliated. These people have not been converted from one position to the other; they just couldn't care less about distinctions which to them are insignificant. Our ministers know this too. For more than a generation they have felt increasing embarrassment about preaching on their inherited peculiarities as issues of major importance; and many of them no longer treat them at all. Our denominational officials know this. To them the denomination is simply the ecclesiastical machine with which they are called to work. The world knows this. If it listens to Martin Luther King, for example, it is because it recognizes in him some-thing relevantly Christian, not because he is a Baptist. If the general public inquires about the President's religion, it wants as-surance that he is a man of conviction and integrity and prayer; it has no interest in keeping a box score on whether he attended the Christian Church or the Episcopal Church last Sunday. We all know that our denominational separation is irrelevant and anachro-nistic, and the pretense that issues of tremendous importance are in-volved smacks of hypocrisy.

This is not to say that we should not love the communion to which we now belong. In God's good providence "our" com-munion has brought us the knowledge of Christ, surrounded us with inspiring fellowship, given us our opportunity for ministry. This is not to say that we should be cynical about the work and the structures of our denominations; if we are going to labor for

111

the Lord in our time we must work with these instrumentalities; it would be foolish to set up more. This is not to say that the particular traditions of our denominations are meaningless or shameful; in each one we have received a goodly heritage which we rightly prize. The point is that there is no justification for perpetuating the multiplicity of our divisions. The only reason for allowing them to continue is the difficulty of doing something about them.

Here then the effort to establish a reunited church truly catholic, truly evangelical, and truly reformed becomes, I believe, a divine mandate in our day. The proposal is genuinely ecumenical in conception in that it seeks to gather up what is right and significant in our various separated traditions and to bring them into the common treasury of the reconstituted fellowship. Obviously the union of six denominations, if successful, does not cancel all the evils of the denominational system. But it should send a thrill of accomplishment through American Protestantism. It should pave the way for even more inclusive union. It should gather now-separated Christians together in many a community and help to overcome much of the meaningless dissipation of our resources as we seek to bear a Christian witness to a needy world.

V

The fourth area of needed reformation is in the realm of mission. The church's calling is not to serve her own institutional ends but to bring the good news of God to the life of the world and to minister to mankind in its varied need.

Martin Luther's understanding of original sin was the natural man's characteristic self-preoccupation; his interests are turned inward upon himself (*incurvatus in se*).[1] This demonic self-love, this unhealthy introversion, this sin which clings so closely, constantly threatens to ensnare the church of God. We are caught in its toils today. A new sanctuary for our congregation, a new organ, stained-glass windows, plush carpeting for the aisles, a paved parking lot, a campsite for our youth, an apartment house for our "golden age" members—we can raise money for these. Money for missions and for ministering to the world's need comes so much harder. The ministry, sacraments, liturgy, the Word of God, tradition—we can preempt the energies of our major theologians for a generation on such churchly topics. It is not so easy to get men intellectually excited over formulating a Christian witness to the issues that threaten the future of mankind. Reorganization of the congregation, enlarging the state staff, restructuring the denomination, overhauling the National Council and the World Council, even (I will say it) working on a plan of church union—we bend our efforts and our thoughts to these enterprises.

But the struggle for civil rights, the plight of our nation's poor, the bitter aimlessness of youth, the pathetic efforts of underdeveloped nations to achieve freedom and abundance for their people—we are not sure that the church should weaken her influence or threaten her program by getting involved in such controversial matters. E. R. Wickham speaks shockingly but perhaps not too strongly when he writes,

May we not say that God in his mercy will not allow the world to come into the Church as she now is? That it would be dreadful if our churches as at present conditioned were thronged with people seeking membership? May it not be that God will not allow the Church to convert the world, unless the Church is adequate to the needs of the world—that He won't let us succeed at the wrong task.[2]

The parable of the talents speaks a stern warning. The condemnation of the wicked and slothful servant may well fall upon us who have buried the Lord's resources within the church walls, when our duty is to put them to work in carrying out his business. A church truly reformed is a church ever responsive to the voice of her master: "The Son of man came not to be served but to serve" (Mark 10:45).

VI

Ecclesia reformata semper reformanda. A church truly reformed can never be content with herself, her glorious tradition, her impressive accomplishments, the esteem in which she is held. "Yet once more," says the Lord, "I will shake the heavens and the earth" (see Heb. 12:26). And in that terrible earthquake of divine judgment the church must be not only willing but eager to see everything lost which God can shake loose. So when the ground beneath us begins to rock, let us not fear. Rather let us give thanks that we have received a kingdom which cannot be shaken—a church truly reformed.

PART IV
A Church Truly Catholic

CHAPTER 7
The Communion of Saints

In the building of a church sufficient to these times, we are ever guided by the vision of the towers gleaming in the light. We have summarized the vision in a trinity of qualities—a church truly evangelical, a church truly reformed, a church truly catholic. We begin now our consideration of the third descriptive phrase.

It should hardly be necessary any longer to point out that the term *catholic,* as it is being used here, is not to be confused with the title of a particular Christian communion, the Roman Catholic Church. Certainly it is not to be limited to that body. Many other majestic and inclusive Christian names have been incorporated into the official titles of particular churches—Evangelical, Reformed, Orthodox, Pentecostal, Christian—but the rest of Christendom still retains the right to use them in their broad and original intent as referring to essential qualities of the true church wherever it may be found. Hosts of Protestants who confess the Apostles' Creed affirm every Sunday their belief in "the holy catholic church." The argument of this book is that every church—not just those denominations which happen to bear one of the adjectives in their official title—is called to be truly evangelical, truly reformed, truly catholic. While the churches in the Consultation on Church Union are non-Roman, we do not wish to be anti-Roman in any vindictive sense. But to us, "catholic" is not a synonym for "papal."

What then does it mean to say "a church truly catholic"?

Catholicity implies all that makes for the wholeness of the church. It presents the picture of the church both growing toward perfection and also manifesting that perfection of oneness, holiness, and apostolicity which already interpenetrates the ambiguities of her earthly life. The word carries the meaning of *universality* in geographical extent; of *inclusiveness* of all sorts and conditions, all ranks and races of men who confess the name of Christ; of *continuity* with the generations of the faithful who have gone before us; of *communion* with the risen Lord. (Thus the worship of any Christian congregation is caught up with the offering of praise rising from the entire company of the church militant on earth and that in turn mingles with the continual liturgy of the church triumphant in a glorious eucharist transcending space and time.) Catholicity suggests *orthodoxy,* to be thought of in ideal terms not as an official definition of dogma but as that essential body of belief, implicit in the gospel, which constitutes the faith confessed by all Christians everywhere and in every generation: (the formula comes from Vincent of Lérins) *ubique, semper, ab omnibus.* Thus catholicity embraces the prophetic genius of Protestantism for a faithful witness to the gospel of Christ who is Lord of all being, King of kings, and head over his body the church.

Obviously when we speak of catholicity in all the richness of its connotation we are discussing not an attribute of the church but rather the essential nature of the church itself. It is clear why any true church must be truly catholic.

I

Yet despite the inclusive vision, the people of God who profess their participation in the holy catholic church and in the communion of saints repeatedly find themselves sundered one from another by every sort of historical circumstance and cultural barrier. Variations in practice quickly develop which, to the rigid minds of some, cannot be regarded as legitimate diversity but rather as illicit departure from the truth. The church has never been free from such tendencies, even in New Testament times, as John Knox points out in *The Early Church and the Coming Great Church.* The quest for catholicity is as old as the Christian community itself.

In a fascinating historical parallel Knox compares the "early catholic" movement of the second century with the ecumenical movement of our own era. His discussion of the instruments of unity developed by the second-century bishops is particularly pertinent to our present discussion. These were a catholic canon of authoritative books setting forth the gospel of Christ (our New Testament), a catholic confession of faith (The Apostles' Creed in its essential outline), and a catholic order (episcopacy). While these instruments were not fully developed until the fourth century, Knox maintains, they were well established by A.D. 200 and must be taken seriously by anyone presently concerned with the oneness of the church. The argument derives cogency from John Knox's impartial scholarship; his position emerges from his biblical and historical studies, not from the particular Christian tradition in which he was nurtured.

One of the most important attempts of an ecclesiastical body to put forth an official pronouncement concerning the elements of catholicity resulted in the much-discussed Chicago-Lambeth Quadrilateral of 1888. Issued by the world conference of Anglican bishops, the document essays to set forth "the principles of unity exemplified by the undivided Catholic Church during the first ages of its existence." It offers these principles as the basis on which Anglicans are willing to enter into discussion with other Christian communions. The four points of the Quadrilateral, originally drafted by Bishop Huntington of the Protestant Episcopal Church in the United States in 1870 and adopted by the American House of Bishops in 1886, are as follows:

(a) The Holy Scriptures of the Old and New Testaments, as "containing all things necessary to salvation," and as being the rule and ultimate standard of faith.

(b) The Apostles' Creed, as the Baptismal Symbol; and the Nicene Creed, as the sufficient statement of the Christian Faith.

(c) The two Sacraments ordained by Christ Himself—Baptism and the Supper of the Lord—ministered with unfailing use of Christ's words of institution and of the elements ordained by Him.

(d) The Historic Episcopate, locally adapted in the methods of its administration to the varying needs of the nations and peoples called of God into the unity of His Church.[1]

While the intention of the bishops in promulgating these four principles was undoubtedly catholic, many Protestants have tended to regard the Quadrilateral as a partisan document, particularly in point (d). Free churchmen and liberals fancy themselves as bound to object also to point (b). Such resistance would seem to indicate hypersensitivity. My own communion for example likes to regard itself as the freest among left-wing Protestants, and many Disciples have nursed a particular allergy toward creeds, at least until quite recent years. It is noteworthy, in the light of such attitudes, that as early as 1853 Alexander Campbell offered to the Christian world at least three of the points of the later Chicago-Lambeth Quadrilateral. In *Christian Baptism* he wrote as follows:

We have proposed an *Evangelical Reformation*—or, rather, a return to the faith and manners anciently delivered to the saints—A RESTORATION *of original Christianity both in theory and practice*. The three capital points of which are:—

    I. The Christian Scriptures, the only rule and measure of Christian faith and learning.

    II. The Christian confession, the foundation of Christian union and communion.

    III. The Christian ordinances—baptism, the Lord's day, and the Lord's supper,—as taught and observed by the Apostles.[2]

Here is an instructive parallel.

Both proposals agree in their first point, the Holy Scriptures.

Both agree in placing the Christian confession second. While the ways of expressing this statement differ, the implicit variance in substance is not so great as some may imagine. Disciples have been content to use biblical confessions (particularly Matt. 16:16), but Campbell elsewhere expressed his full assent to the Apostles' Creed.[3] The later metaphysical creeds (including the creed commonly called Nicene) Disciples have regarded as speculative and divisive, yet Campbell's faith was essentially that of "Nicea." (This creed is reproduced later in this chapter.)

In their third statements, both proposals emphasize baptism and eucharist, though regarding baptism, some ground for discussion remains concerning the condition, "as taught and observed by the Apostles."

Campbell's proposal contains no fourth item comparable to the Lambeth statement on the "Historic Episcopate." Yet it is significant that elsewhere he referred to his efforts "to contend for the original faith and order."[4] Disciples generally regard the historic

121

episcopate as having emerged in the postapostolic age and consequently as not being a part of the "original . . . order."

The various points of traditional disagreement are subject to fresh examination in the light of recent biblical and historical studies and the new ecumenical climate. The striking fact about these two statements from traditions sometimes thought to be far apart is the close parallels between them and the fact that both register concern for the wholeness of the church, both single out the same areas of emphasis in their approach to the problem of unity.

It should be frankly acknowledged that in setting forth his proposal for a church truly catholic and truly reformed, Eugene Carson Blake tacitly accepted the terms of the Lambeth Quadrilateral, although he did not mention it by name. As I conceive the genius of his move, it was not to commit Presbyterians and others to these terms in advance; he could not do that. Rather it was to say: Let us for once seriously discuss the possibility of a united church in these terms and see what it would look like. I believe that it would look acceptable to him, as I believe it would to me, and to many others. So the work of the Consultation continues in the effort to sketch the outlines of a reunited church. You will remember that the catholic principles which Blake indicated as important to his proposal are (a) "visible and historical continuity with the Church of all ages" accepting bishops in the historic succession, (b) "the historic trinitarian faith . . . set forth in the Apostles' and Nicene Creeds," and (c) "the two sacraments, instituted by Christ." The point about the Holy Scriptures he included under the reformed elements in his proposal.

A major effort toward the reunion of Christ's church is therefore now under way in this country, presumably bound to take seriously the Chicago-Lambeth conception of catholicity. Any discussion of a church truly catholic which ignored the issues raised by the Quadrilateral would be something less than realistic. Already we have discussed the Holy Scriptures (Chap. 5) and the sacraments (all too briefly in Chap. 3). In the rest of this chapter I intend to look briefly at the question of "visible and historical continuity with the Church of all ages," [5] particularly as this refers to the historic succession of bishops and "the historic trinitarian faith." In the two succeeding chapters it is my purpose to indicate certain implications of catholicity which are of utmost importance and which we dare not lose sight of in preoccupation with one or two thorny issues just indicated. Chap. 8 will deal with the visible unity of the church within geographical areas. Chap. 9 will address itself to a fundamental aspect of catholicity too often overlooked—its purpose, which is to enable the church in its wholeness to be meaningfully related in service to the whole world. Ultimately the church's catholicity must be a manifestation to the world of life under the lordship of Christ, or it is to no avail.

II

A church truly catholic will give meaningful expression to its continuity with the church of all ages.

The American experience of setting sail for a New World, of finding our national unity in a rebellion against the Old, of participating in an ethos which emerged during the height of the belief in progress toward new and greater things has inevitably stunted our sense of proper indebtedness to the generations that went long before. We have taken with implicit faith Walt Whitman's stirring lines:

> All the past we leave behind . . .
> Pioneers! O pioneers!

This mentality, this assumption that everything really significant belongs to the present or the future, has unconsciously distorted the understanding of American Christians toward the church's past and blinded us to the important role which a sense of continuity with all the people of God in every generation plays in the concept of catholicity. Many of the old churches of Europe are built on the spot where the first missionary to a given community was martyred. The popular piety cherishes relics of the saints and the physical ruins of the past in a manner that sometimes threatens to turn the church into a museum of antiquities. But a concern for continuity cannot be dismissed as mere antiquarianism.

I cherish the recollection of a memorable conversation in Thessalonica with the gracious Orthodox bishop of that place: He said with quiet earnestness, "It is a great responsibility to be the bishop of a church founded by the apostle Paul." Talk about New Testament Christianity!

The present concern in the Faith and Order discussions with Tradition and the recognition that Tradition is not some secret body of dogma to be set over against the Scriptures but rather "the living stream of the Church's life" indicates a wholesome recovery throughout Christendom of the concept of continuity. We have already observed how the Bible itself, the symbol of the church truly reformed, is at the same time a major instrument of continuity within the Christian fellowship.

The same may be said for the liturgy, particularly for the use of some of the words and phrases repeated by every generation of Christians from the apostles to ourselves: *Amen, Alleluia, Kyrie eleison, Maranatha, Abba, Father*. In these instances the very words of the earliest church have come down to us untranslated from the original Hebrew or Greek or Aramaic, though the pronunciation may have been corrupted!

Almost as ancient are many of our ascriptions of praise: the doxology added to the Lord's Prayer, the *Gloria Patri,* the *Gloria Tibi.* Then come the hymns: some from the Hebrew Psalter, some like the *Benedictus* and the *Magnificat* from the worship of the earliest church, and some added to the treasury of sacred song out of every century of Christian history. So with the ancient rites—baptism, the breaking of bread, the laying on of hands, the processional hymn; or the familiar symbols—the Chi Rho, the IHS, the lamb, the fish, the crown, and "the cross of Jesus going on before." Every worshiping congregation of Christians participates in the catholicity which is the continuity of the church. Occasionally a sudden intensity of insight into the meaning of this communion with all the saints must overwhelm us on even the most ordinary occasion of worship, causing each of us to square his shoulders and straighten his spine and sending us marching out boldly to our unfinished task:

> Like a mighty army
> Moves the Church of God,
> Brothers, we are treading
> Where the saints have trod.

The catholicity of the church as a continuing community of believers is thus implicit in every service of Christian worship. Our opportunity is great, however, to enter more fully into the realization of our position in the "endless line of splendor" which is the worshiping and witnessing church. This means constant work in teaching our congregations the meaning of the actions, symbols, hymns, and responses which we use in the corporate praise of God. We may profit from studying other liturgical forms besides those of our own tradition and then from joining in worship according to those orders. One of the benefits to be foreseen in the achievement of a reunited church such as is sought by the Consultation on Church Union is the enrichment of our particular liturgical inheritances by the practices of the other communions. With such distinctive patterns of worship as now prevail among the six member

125

bodies, it is hardly to be desired that *one* official order be immediately developed for uniform use in all the congregations. Rather the service book of the new church might well contain alternate orders, representative of the best in each of the traditions. A given congregation could thus arrange to use in the course of the year not only that pattern to which it is accustomed by long usage, but also each of the other orders, so that the fullness of its participation in the catholicity of Christian devotion might be enlarged.

The emergence of church history as an academic discipline within the colleges and seminaries of the American free churches during recent generations has done something to develop a greater awareness of continuity with the church of all the ages. I shall be forever grateful for the privilege that was mine of studying history at the University of Oregon under one of the great medievalists, Quirinus Breen, whose own sense of our involvement in the past and whose rigorous assignments in the great authors of antiquity, the Middle Ages, the Renaissance, and Reformation provided me with a basis for understanding the continuity of the church. One of the remarkable transformations of church history in recent decades has been its fading as an instrument of denominational apologetics and its emergence as an ecumenical force, a handmaiden of catholicity.

The dramatization of continuity is one of the benefits of the historic episcopate. We may be permitted (along with many faithful Episcopalians) our reservations about the verifiability of an unbroken line of bishops going back to the apostles, just as we can raise minor skeptical objections to almost any Christian symbol or practice. But the point of the symbol comes through. In more than one ancient parish in the British Isles I have reverently read the plaque in the narthex setting forth the name of every pastor back to the church's foundation, perhaps a thousand years ago.

Other elements of continuity also deserve recognition. The church is not the clergy but the whole company of the people of

God, and there is a continuity of membership, of humble and devout men and women who lived and died by the faith, across all the generations. No one can be skeptical about that. The line of this continuity is difficult to trace in the records, for it involves "a great multitude which no man could number." But it stands back of the life of every community of Christians in the world today. Nor is it as inchoate as it may first appear.

Douglas Horton, in a little book on Congregationalism, advances a dramatic and moving interpretation of the continuity of congregations.[6] The living stream of the church's life has flowed through objective historical channels from Jesus Christ to ourselves: the reality of visible communities of believers bound together and to their Lord in holy covenant and faithfully imparting to those who came after them the treasure of the received faith. Given congregations rise and pass away, like all the generations of men, but they are, says Horton, the essential element in the continuity of the church and so every one of them in some measure manifests its catholicity.

III

And what of the continuity of the faith in the sense of an authentic understanding of the gospel by which believers are brought to a true knowledge of God in Christ? We must simply acknowledge here that for the vast majority of Christians this continuity of belief is symbolized in the ancient creeds. The left-wing churches of Protestantism have for the most part elected not to use the creeds, not from a wish to deny them but from the fear that they might usurp the sole authority of the Scripture in such matters, or could not be understood by the laity, or threatened Christian freedom. In these days, it would seem that some in the creedless churches can scarcely say what they believe themselves and don't want anyone else telling them what they are supposed to believe!

How then are we to understand the proposal that the "reunited Church must clearly confess the historic trinitarian faith received from the Apostles and set forth in the Apostles' and Nicene Creeds?" That way of stating it seems a bit more rigid than the terms of the Quadrilateral itself: "The Apostles' Creed, as the Baptismal Symbol; and the Nicene Creed, as the sufficient statement of the Christian faith."

The place of creeds in the life of a reunited church must be faced realistically. It is inconceivable to me, though apparently it was not to my direct spiritual forebears, that the great body of Christians, even of Protestants, should entertain thoughts of abandoning the ancient creeds. It is equally evident that these same Christians who cherish the creeds are as fully committed to Christian liberty as are my fellow Disciples. They fear them no more than any other authentic proclamation of the faith. So far as I can discern, the Constitution of the United Church of Christ accurately reflects the prevailing attitude:

The United Church of Christ . . . claims as its own the faith of the historic Church expressed in the ancient creeds and reclaimed in the basic insights of the Protestant Reformers. It affirms the responsibility of the Church in each generation to make this faith its own in reality of worship, in honesty of thought and expression, and in purity of heart before God.

Douglas Horton's forthright observation on the ancient creeds and their place in the United Church of Christ should clarify the issue for many:

Although these creeds may not seem to all today . . . to express the truth in every line, they contain, in relatively simple form, a statement of Christian essentials that are the same yesterday, today, and forever. Granted that they also may contain single sentences or phrases that some critical minds of today, disciplined to seek the truth in Christ's name, cannot accept, these are like the incidental folklore and unchristian vagaries of the authors of the Bible; they do not prevent the broader and essential truth about God from shining through the whole.[7]

When the texts of the creeds are considered, their function as proclamatory anthems, singing forth the glory of the gospel, is evident. The so-called Apostles' Creed, for example, is a brief summary of the faith used by the second-century church in Rome to instruct candidates for baptism:

I believe in God the Father Almighty, Maker of heaven and earth:

And in Jesus Christ his only Son our Lord: Who was conceived by the Holy Ghost, Born of the Virgin Mary: Suffered under Pontius Pilate, Was crucified, dead, and buried: He descended into hell; The third day he rose again from the dead: He ascended into heaven, And sitteth on the right hand of God the Father Almighty: From thence he shall come to judge the quick and the dead.

I believe in the Holy Ghost: The holy Catholic Church; The Communion of Saints: The Forgiveness of sins: The Resurrection of the body: And the Life everlasting. Amen.

The Nicene Creed is a fourth-century elaboration of the earlier formula.

Transcending by its majesty the bitterness of ancient controversy and even the limitations of the Greek metaphysical terminology in which it is couched, it resounds through the centuries as a stirring paean of praise to the only-begotten Son of God:

I believe in one God the Father Almighty, Maker of heaven and earth, And of all things visible and invisible:

And in one Lord Jesus Christ, the only-begotten Son of God; begotten of the Father before all worlds, God of God, Light of Light, Very

God of very God, Begotten, not made; Being of one substance with the Father; By whom all things were made: Who for us men and for our salvation came down from heaven, And was incarnate by the Holy Ghost of the Virgin Mary, And was made man: And was crucified also for us under Pontius Pilate; He suffered and was buried: And the third day he rose again according to the Scriptures: And ascended into heaven, And sitteth on the right hand of the Father: and he shall come again, with glory, to judge both the quick and the dead; Whose kingdom shall have no end.

And I believe in the Holy Ghost, The Lord, and Giver of Life, Who proceedeth from the Father and the Son; Who with the Father and the Son together is worshipped and glorified; Who spake by the Prophets: And I believe one Catholic and Apostolic Church: I acknowledge one Baptism for the remission of sins: And I look for the Resurrection of the dead: And the Life of the world to come. Amen.

A stirring contemporary proclamation of the good news is the Statement of Faith confessed by the United Church of Christ. It was written by a special commission of that church appointed at the time of union, and was adopted for voluntary use by the second General Synod. It has gained wide acceptance throughout the Christian world.

We believe in God, the Eternal Spirit, Father of our Lord Jesus Christ and our Father, and to his deeds we testify:

> He calls the worlds into being,
>   creates man in his own image
>   and sets before him the ways of life and death.

> He seeks in holy love to save all people from
>   aimlessness and sin.

> He judges men and nations by his righteous will
>   declared through prophets and apostles.

130

In Jesus Christ, the man of Nazareth, our crucified
 and risen Lord,
 he has come to us
 and shared our common lot,
 conquering sin and death
 and reconciling the world to himself.

He bestows upon us his Holy Spirit,
 creating and renewing the Church of Jesus Christ,
 binding in covenant faithful people of all ages,
  tongues, and races.

He calls us into his Church
 to accept the cost and joy of discipleship,
 to be his servants in the service of men,
 to proclaim the gospel to all the world
 and resist the powers of evil,
 to share in Christ's baptism and eat at his table,
 to join in his passion and victory.

He promises to all who trust him
 forgiveness of sins and fullness of grace,
 courage in the struggle for justice and peace,
 his presence in trial and rejoicing,
 and eternal life in his kingdom which has no end.

Blessing and honor, glory and power be unto him. Amen.

Considering the way in which these affirmations are now used to
proclaim the historic faith, no one should have real difficulty in
accepting such creeds within the life of a reunited church. No union
of scope, I am convinced, will be achieved without these great corporate testimonies. I must confess that I have attended enough
services of worship at ecumenical meetings that I find the unison

declaration of the Apostles' Creed a meaningful act of witness. And I find increasingly that the Nicene Creed is a majestic affirmation of the gospel as I understand it and have attempted to set it forth in Chap. 2. No one intends now to use the creeds as instruments of persecution. They are, within the continuity of the church, towering witnesses to the catholic faith. "This is the victory that overcomes the world" (I John 5:4). Go tell it on the mountain!

CHAPTER 8
Knit Together for Growth and Love

At one essential point our Christianity differs radically from anything known in the church for its first fifteen hundred years. I refer to our assumption that it is normal and proper for Christians in the same community to be separated from one another.

Until recent times the divisions which troubled Christendom followed geographical lines. The Eastern patriarchs and the Roman bishop broke fellowship in the eleventh century, and their souls have been troubled—rightly so—ever since, but that schism did not rupture the witness and fellowship of most Christians where they lived. Similarly, in the sixteenth century, reformation took place, where it was successful, through national churches. So each of the princely or ducal realms of Germany remained with the pope or went with Luther according to the faith of its ruler (*cujus regio, ejus religio*). The church in one after another of the Swiss cantons was reformed. The Church of Sweden accepted the Lutheran reformation. The Church of England set up its own spiritual household. The Church of Scotland followed Knox into Presbyterianism. France, Spain, and Italy remained Roman Catholic. Now I do not overlook the role of the civil state in enforcing religious uniformity in the various realms; nevertheless in the thinking and experience of most Christians, the church in their locality remained united. Nations fought one another in the wars of religion, but a good Scots Presbyterian never came in contact with an Episcopalian except on those distasteful occasions when he met an Englishman. All this is to say that until the last four hundred years Christians did not know themselves to be divided locally.

The major exception to this generalization is the era of heresy and schism in the history of the ancient church; then you had two groups, each claiming to be the true church, sometimes living side by side. But in those days, at least one of them anathematized the other, for it held that so grievous a departure from the faith or order of the true church could in no way be countenanced. Thus both heresy and schism were gravely reprehended as threatening the truth of the faith and the unity of Christians.

Our present situation arose as the anomalous accompaniment of modern religious liberty. In the intellectual ferment of the seventeenth century, governments found it increasingly difficult to maintain religious uniformity, and with the influence of the eighteenth-century Enlightenment, toleration became general. The multiplication of sects was rapid, particularly in the United States where, with limited and brief exceptions, religious establishment was not known and churches could compete on an equal footing. For a little while the official doctrine of each church tended to regard all the others as heretics, but that attitude soon gave way to toleration.

Thus we blithely endure a situation, more incredible to our spiritual ancestors than rocket voyages to the moon, in which members of different denominations in the same community virtually ignore one another as Christians. We do business together. Our children attend the same schools. We meet one another at ball games and political rallies. Our families intermarry. But even though we may not care a scrap for the differences between our churches, we do not break bread together at the Lord's table; indeed the rules of our churches may forbid us to do so. We do not bear a common Christian witness together in the life of our community because, while we may know one another as decent citizens and may be informed as to one another's church membership, we have no churchly experience together. If we pray together, it is likely to be at a football game or a luncheon club or other public occasion, or in an informally arranged devotional meeting, not under the auspices of the church.

How utterly intolerable such a situation, which we take for granted, would have seemed to the Apostle Paul! How agitated he became at any suggestion that Jewish Christians should not worship with and eat with Gentile Christians in the same place. This was the issue over which he withstood Peter "eyeball to eyeball"! What does it mean to confess one holy catholic church when the confessing congregation ignores other congregations making the same confession in the same community?

A current ecumenical watchword is "All in each place, one." It summarizes the ideal of unity endorsed by the New Delhi Assembly of the World Council of Churches in December, 1961:

We believe that the unity which is both God's will and his gift to his Church is being made visible as all in each place who are baptized into Jesus Christ and confess him as Lord and Saviour are brought by the Holy Spirit into ONE fully committed fellowship, holding the one apostolic faith, preaching the one Gospel, breaking the one bread, joining in common prayer, and having a corporate life reaching out in witness and service to all and who at the same time are united with the whole Christian fellowship in all places and all ages in such wise that ministry and members are accepted by all, and that all can act and speak together as occasion requires for the tasks to which God calls his people.[1]

This is an eloquent and pointed statement which ought to be explored together by Christians in every community. For catholicity begins at home. And that is where our denial of catholicity is most flagrant and most damaging.

One of the most appealing aspects of the task which the participating churches have assigned to the Consultation on Church Union is the possibility of recovering catholicity in many communities. I know of small towns even now where two or more struggling congregations want to unite but are hindered by the separation of their respective denominations. Such a union as the Consultation envisages would not be just a "merger at the top." It would enable many such congregations to find their oneness, to experience catholicity at a new depth, and to witness far more authentically in their communities. Whether through this scheme or other breakthroughs to be worked out locally, a major imperative is to realize the catholicity of the church where people live. We are called to manifest the oneness of all Christians in each place.

I

The need for the oneness of Christians goes beyond the local community. A church truly catholic must seek to develop and maintain a Christian structure of cohesion among the congregations.

The text for this thesis is Eph. 4:15-16: "We are to grow up in every way into him who is the head, into Christ, from whom the whole body, joined and knit together by every joint with which it is supplied, when each part is working properly, makes bodily growth and upbuilds itself in love."

136

What are the joints and ligaments which provide cohesion for the body of Christ on earth? In the earliest days of the church they appear to have been quite informal, but nevertheless deliberate and essential. The frequent visits among the churches by apostles, missionaries, and evangelists, the letters of admonition and counsel (some of which constitute part of our New Testament), the offerings by which Christians of one region shared in the needs of their suffering brethren, the practice of hospitality which drew Christians who were traveling to the homes of their fellow believers—all these were expressions of the church's catholicity. In a fascinating way, most of these procedures were reproduced by the churches moving westward on the American frontier. Substitute the religious journal for the epistle and you have a remarkable similarity. In the greater complexity of modern urban life, some of the old informal devices are not so effective as they once were. But the need for joints and ligaments is just as great.

Here is a major function of the ordained ministry within the church. Writing as a Congregationalist, Daniel Jenkins has pointed out that one of the distinctive characteristics of the minister is at this point: He represents the great church to the congregation he serves.[2] We tend to lose sight of this, because we think of a congregation as calling a minister, ordaining him if necessary, employing him as its servant, and then sending him on his way when his service is done. It is important to remember that in nearly every case the minister has been reared and nurtured elsewhere, that he has been educated by the church at large, that he probably has been ordained elsewhere, so that he is not just the creature of the congregation he serves. His experience, his education, and (let us hope) his theological principles bring constantly into the life of his people the broader perspective of the church at large. In even the most fiercely congregational churches, the ministry has this representative character; the only way to avoid it would be to appoint no one as minister except a longtime member of the congregation uncorrupted by experience or education outside. The fact that few congregations would settle for such a leadership underscores the importance of the ministry as an instrument of catholicity.

Congregationally ordered churches are now coming to realize that each congregation therefore has a stake in the ministry at large, not just in the man who happens to be serving it at this time. This is a major reason for the formal connectional structure prevailing in other churches, whether presbyteries, synods, conferences, conventions, or the personal link of bishops.[3] In a number of states my own congregationally governed communion is now seeking to give expression to a more organic concept of the relationship among the churches; instead of state missionary societies we are speaking forthrightly of associations of churches or simply calling ourselves the Christian Churches (Disciples of Christ) in a given area. One of the most important attendant developments is the growth of state commissions on the ministry. In some places these commissions have become at least semipresbyterian in function. Thus the experience of all the churches demonstrates the importance of the ministry in binding together the body of Christ. Hence the body as a whole, and not merely the congregation served by a particular minister, manifests a concern for and discipline over the ministry. The Presbyterian churches and the Methodist Church have developed careful and efficient systems for the ordering of the ministry. But even those communions which once attempted to avoid every suggestion of ecclesiasticism are seeking structures by which they may act responsibly in such a matter of common concern.

II

In reflecting on the church's wholeness, we must acknowledge the strong appeal in the conception of the ministry as ordered about the bishop, a shepherd of the Christian flock and especially the spiritual counselor of the clergy in a limited geographical area. A most persuasive exposition of this conception is advanced by Theodore Otto Wedel, in his book, *The Coming Great Church*. A bishop symbolizes in his person the unity of the ministry in his diocese and through his fellowship with other bishops the oneness of the churches in all the dioceses; he can be consecrated only when three other bishops are present. Thus order is safeguarded and the succession of bishops down the generations is dramatized.

So far there has been only preliminary conversation about these matters in the Consultation on Church Union. The strong preponderance of opinion is to think of the bishop in pastoral rather than administrative terms. It is assumed that the diocese should be comparatively small (as it was in the ancient church when the bishop was a local pastor, not the administrator of a vast missionary province). I gather that a diocese in the reunited church might well take in territory comparable to that of a presbytery or a Methodist conference today, with perhaps one diocese for every two hundred congregations. Hence the bishops would be men close to their pastors and churches, with minimal temptations to pomp and circumstance. They would be too numerous to be oddities. (A seminary dean, by contrast, would be a rare bird!)

While members of non-Episcopal churches have often looked cordially on such a possibility, the hottest issue in union negotiations has regularly been the question of reordination. Churches without the historic episcopate have not been willing to concede that their ministries have been invalid. The union in South India was the first great breakthrough on this score; the ministries of all the uniting churches were accepted without reordination, along with bishops in the historic succession. Something similar appears to be possible in the discussions thus far within the Consultation. At the time of union all the ministries would be reconsecrated to the fuller ministry of the reunited church, but this act would not call into question the validity of their previous ordination except to recognize with gratitude the wider opportunity for ministry now to be available.

Such thinking as this is new to many ministers and laymen in nonepiscopal churches. And because it is new it is at least mildly frightening. But it is worth our pondering. For here is an authentically Christian, spiritually meaningful conception of the joints and ligaments among the churches. Over against that is the danger of a purely pragmatic connectional structure designed in imitation of secular procedures—"addressograph" lists, IBM cards, and all the paraphernalia of mass communication. Such devices should be consecrated to the divine mission, but I find myself increasingly repelled by a connectional structure which is basically promotional, its chief minister reduced to the role of an executive secretary or production manager. A church truly catholic will seek a structure of cohesion which in itself witnesses to the redemptive fellowship given through the gospel. We shall do well to consider carefully the pastoral office of bishop.

I confess that it has taken some years for me to reach this position and that at times I have found myself moving towards it almost in spite of myself. My commitment as a Disciple to the conception of the universal priesthood of the whole people of God, which my first experiences in the Faith and Order movement drove me to affirm with an almost frantic earnestness, remains undiminished. But I now see this sort of pastoral episcopacy as in no sense conflicting with but rather as reinforcing the common ministry of all the believers. The more I have reflected on the necessity for organic cohesion within the church at large, whether my thinking was directed toward the specific problems of my own communion or the broader question of Christian unity, the more persuasive the possibilities in episcopacy have appeared.

This is not to deny at all the legitimacy of other instruments of cohesion through which *episkope,* shepherding oversight, is actually exercised: the presbytery, the conference, the responsible commitment of mutual concern which characterizes congregational polity at its best. Surely the values in these forms of *episkope* must be retained for a united church. But it is apparent that increasing numbers of churchmen in the various communions are coming to a concept of reunion which involves pastoral bishops in historic succession.

My one reservation respects the danger of the negative inference, a tendency which threatens every positive value in the Christian scheme. The Jews knew themselves to be the chosen people of God; the negative (and mistaken) inference was that God had rejected all others. Christians through the centuries have gratefully found the sacraments a means of grace; the negative inference concluded that in the absence of the sacraments, or even of the sacraments "rightly administered," grace is automatically withheld. Christians in every generation have joyfully confessed that in their experience of Jesus Christ they have been brought into the saving knowledge of God; the negative inference has been that no one might know God except through Jesus Christ. I say reverently and carefully that in none of these instances dare we draw the negative inference. Our task is to proclaim joyfully the positive affirmation in the sure faith that it will be used of God for all the healing virtue that is in it.

So with the historic episcopacy. Many of us have been repelled by those of its advocates who majored in the negative inference, that without this particular order, this particular form of churchly cohesion, there is no true church nor valid ministry. We must reject such a view outright. And if ever the providence of God should

141

lead us into a reunited church with pastoral bishops, we must resist the temptation both to conscious pride and to unconscious arrogance. We must never deny the validity of other ministries simply because they do not share in this particular order; we must never exclude other communions from our conception of the church catholic on the ground of a presumed deficiency at this point. Eugene Carson Blake guards against any such negative inference in his proposal that

without adopting any particular theory of historic succession, the reunited Church shall provide at its inception for the consecration of all its bishops by bishops and presbyters both in the apostolic succession and out of it from all over the world from all Christian churches which would authorize or permit them to take part.[4]

On such terms we should gladly consider the role of pastoral bishops in a united church. We should seek for those forms of catholicity which, without negating the gospel and the freedom that is in Christ, serve as the most effective and spiritually authentic ligaments of cohesion within his body on this earth.

III

And what of the relationships which extend beyond the reach of any particular communion, or even of a reunited church so thrillingly inclusive as that sought by the Consultation on Church Union? These too constitute an aspect of catholicity, even though the instruments for expressing them (councils of churches [5] and other cooperative bodies) are new and cumbersome, even though they lack the sanctity of tradition and are removed from the experience of the average members in the congregation. We are nevertheless being granted through them new realizations of the catholic character of the church.

On a memorable evening at Montreal during the Fourth World Conference on Faith and Order an entire session was devoted to our theme. Claude Welch (an American Methodist) read a discerning paper analyzing the "dimensions and demands" of catholicity in the following terms:

1) Catholicity points us to the wholeness of the *truth* in Christ that is to be received and exhibited in the Church. . . .
2) Catholicity orders and intensifies the Church's understanding of mission. . . .
3) Catholicity thus directs attention to the maximal rather than the minimal as the basis for judgment in the church. . . .
4) Finally, catholicity as gift and task refers to every particular church, to the church in every place, however, 'place' may be defined.[6]

Then followed a quiet incident of unforgettable drama: For the first time in the history of the modern ecumenical movement a delegate from the Orthodox Church of Russia came to the rostrum to present a major paper. Archpriest Vitali Borovoy of Leningrad, slated for a discussion of the "Meaning of Catholicity," stood there in his long black robe and began to speak—in English! Struggling with the unfamiliar language—his offering on the ecumenical altar —he spoke in a high-pitched voice strained by nervousness. Yet he showed himself at once a scholar and a Christian. An easy familiarity with the patristic authors characterized his address which moved freely from Greek to Latin to Slavic theologians. His paper presented important insights:

The Church is catholic . . . in the sense of opposing her universal wholeness and catholic unity to all aspects and categories of partial distortion of the fulness of her truth as in various heresies, splits, schisms and every kind of individual fragmentation. . . .

The Catholic Church is not the church of each man separately, nor the church of one see or another, but the church of all in their unity. Understood thus, the catholicity of the Church is not only her inalienable property, but also her basic task. It is not only given to the Church by Christ, but it is also required by Him of all Christians at all times.[7]

When Borovoy finished, with the reference (from Eph. 1:23, KJV) to "the fulness of him that filleth all in all," every Christian present knew that he had experienced one of the great events of his life, one of those rare moments of epiphany when the divine reality he has confessed, though seen in a glass darkly, suddenly shines through. The awareness of participating with a keener consciousness than ever before in the catholicity of the church was sharpened when a member of the Southern Baptist Convention, an accredited visitor but not a delegate, Dale Moody of Louisville, was invited to comment on the previous addresses. With the spontaneity, fervor, and unabashed openness of personal witness characteristic of his people at their best, Moody expounded the concept of the church set forth in Ephesians. Through all this experience none of us could be unmindful of the fraternal interest and prayerful concern of the company of Roman Catholic official observers, sharing more fully in Faith and Order than ever before.

The source of our fuller insight into catholicity that night was not Welch's or Borovoy's or Moody's explanation, though each of them bore faithful and compelling witness. It was the gift of God in making possible in our time the reality of the ecumenical movement, in manifesting through the partial life of all our churches the redemptive wholeness which is in Christ. Here was a company of believers, most of them strangers to one another, gathered from nations long opposed in the hostility of the cold war, from social systems in bitter contest, from diverse cultures, and from confessional traditions, Protestant and Orthodox, which have scarcely ever known, much less understood one another, barely able to speak over the barriers of language and the pain of translation. And yet in that moment there was an acceptance of one another, which took the form of heartfelt and extended applause for Borovoy's paper which people seemed reluctant to stop. In that hour, through the common confession of the lordship of Christ, God had given us a foretaste of the full meaning of catholicity.

This knowledge any worshiping congregation, however humble or undramatic, can share whenever it sings

> Let every kindred, every tribe,
>   On this terrestrial ball,
> To him all majesty ascribe,
>   And crown him Lord of all.
>
> O that, with yonder sacred throng,
>   We at his feet may fall!
> We'll join the everlasting song,
>   And crown him Lord of all.

To join with the whole company of the redeemed, on earth and in heaven, in gratitude for the gospel, in grateful response to the promptings of the Holy Spirit, in manifesting to all mankind the miracle of reconciliation wrought by our Lord Jesus Christ—this is to know the reality of the new people of God gathered by his grace in the truly evangelical, truly reformed, truly catholic church of Christ on earth.

CHAPTER 9

The Wholeness of the Church
for the Wholeness of the World

The elements of catholicity which we have considered up to this point have to do primarily with the inner life of the church. To confine ourselves to such introverted concerns would be to fall into the sin of ecclesiastical self-centeredness and to miss entirely one of the most majestic aspects of catholicity. A church truly catholic under the lordship of Christ will be meaningfully related in its wholeness to the whole world of human concern.

I

The catholicity of the church, so conceived, derives from Christ's lordship over the entire cosmos. Who can forget the magnificent affirmation in the first chapter of Colossians?

He is the image of the invisible God, the first-born of all creation; for in him all things were created, in heaven and on earth, visible and invisible, whether thrones or dominions or principalities or authorities—all things were created through him and for him. He is before all things, and in him all things hold together. He is the head of the body, the church; he is the beginning, the first-born from the dead, that in everything he might be preëminent. For in him all the fullness of God was pleased to dwell, and through him to reconcile to himself all things, whether on earth or in heaven, making peace by the blood of his cross (Col. 1:15-20).

Here is the Christian claim for the lordship of Christ over that vast realm we so often refer to as secular, and here is the charter for the church's involvement in every sphere of the world's life. The catholicity of the church is a manifestation of Christ's lordship, the wholeness of the church's life showing forth the totality of his sovereignty. And since his lordship is confessed first and foremost over the church, wholeness is demanded there. The church's catholicity is sanctified to God as an offering to be used by him for the sake of all the created order. The wholeness of the church becomes a ministry of self-giving for the wholeness of the world. If the true calling of the church is so vast and majestic a vocation, what is the cause of her continuing temptation (and yielding) to the sin of introversion? What lies back of a popular understanding of worship as an experience to be valued because "it makes us feel good"? How can we explain the emphasis in so many congregations on fun and fellowship with "nice people" like ourselves? What is the source of the hesitation to introduce into our common life within the church any proposal that may stir up controversy? Whence springs the widespread reluctance to see the church identified with the great struggles for human dignity going on within our society? How did the church get to be so turned in upon herself?

Whatever the cause—if we may divert for a moment—the result

is quite clear. It is evident in the growing body of literature highly critical of the Christian institution as we know it. In general, we are being told that the church makes little difference in the major decisions which shape our world today. The church is an island of peace and of superficial fellowship in the seas of modern life; nothing much happens there except a few rituals which the members may enjoy but which have little effect on the crucial issues confronting modern man. The church is irrelevant, we are told. Is this really true? And how significant is it that the shortcomings of the church are being set forth by her friends, not her enemies? Can it be that those outside the church scarcely notice her today, even to criticize, and that many of the most thoughtful within her fellowship find the church lacking in true significance?

Certainly much of the criticism is justified. Unless the church of Christ in our time awakens from her lethargy to hear the voice of her Lord calling her from the sin of her introversion, we must concede the argument to the critics. The church *is* irrelevant. And most of what I have written (especially chapters 1, 5, 7, and 9) is inconsequential; in any case it is no *earthly good!* What difference does it make to victims of starvation, to the citizen-slaves of a totalitarian state, to secular existentialists lost in despair, whether the polity of the church is congregational or presbyterian? Whether or not her ministry claims historic succession from the apostles? Whether her liturgy is ordered or free? Whether she reads the Bible or listens to mood music? The judgment of the Lord on such a church has already been spoken in his parable of the barren fig tree: "Why should it use up the ground?" (Luke 13:6-9).

And the cause of this fruitlessness? (We come now to an answer for the series of questions previously stated.) It is clear. The vision of the church is shortsighted, her worship of her Lord timid, her understanding of her calling defective. The introverted church has never really understood the dazzling sweep and unlimited scope of the lordship of Christ—over the church, over society, over the cosmos. She worships a sweet Galilean teacher who died on the cross and perhaps she thinks she believes in his resurrection from the dead. But the church sees this only as his being brought to life again to comfort his disciples. She does not really understand the daring claims of apostolic thought: "And being found in human form he humbled himself and became obedient unto death, even death on a cross" (Phil. 2:8).

What then?

"Therefore God has highly exalted him and bestowed on him the name which is above every name, that at the name of Jesus every knee should bow, in heaven and on earth and under the earth, and every tongue confess that Jesus Christ is Lord, to the glory of God the Father" (Phil. 2:9-11).

A church truly catholic is a church which worships Jesus Christ the Lord of the cosmos, *Christos Pantokrator*. Her wholeness is a manifestation of the integrity of the new creation, the fullness of life which he gives to the community of the reconciled. But it is not a private possession to be enjoyed by God's chosen people in an introverted existence of self-indulgence (not even of spiritual self-indulgence!). The catholicity of the church is a sacred trust to be used for the sake of mankind. Her wholeness is given for the wholeness of the world. How then does the church in the fullness of her catholicity discharge her mission to the whole world under the lordship of Christ?

II

The church truly catholic fully accepts the whole world over which she confesses that Christ is Lord. She teaches that the world is good, that it is important. She recognizes the world as her concern, as the true end of her calling, which is to serve.

The church truly catholic confesses Christ as Lord over the whole order of *creation*. Thereby she gratefully acknowledges all of creation as the handiwork of God, with its divine gifts of abundance and beauty to sustain man's life. She regards as sacred (not as objects of worship but as ordinances of God) the processes of nature in both the subhuman and the human spheres. She concerns herself with the natural needs of mankind—in the name of the Creator who gives seed to the sower and bread to the eater, and of his Son our Lord who instructed his disciples to pray for daily bread. She therefore recognizes as falling within her proper interest the vast enterprises of production through which the resources of earth are processed to meet human needs. She looks upon the whole created world with awe and blesses the reverent inquiry of the scientist into the secrets of the universe.

The church truly catholic confesses Christ as Lord over the whole order of human *life*. She thereby fully accepts all of life as ordained of God and sanctified by Christ. She receives birth and the mysterious process of human mating which leads up to it as the gifts of God. She is concerned for (not that she must conduct or direct) the whole enterprise of education by which little children are guided toward maturity, toward the fullest realization of the possibilities God has placed within them, toward usefulness to mankind. Equally she is concerned with all that makes for meaningful marriage and happy family life. She acknowledges her responsibility toward the deprived, the lonely, the ill, the aged. She is involved with death. Her witness, her worship, her sacraments are intertwined in the totality of man's existence. For the "celebration of life"—its goodness, its meaning, its mystery, its sorrows, its memories—modern man ought not be limited to the devices of musical comedy, or even of those arts which take themselves more seriously. The church catholic in her age-old ritual sanctifies all our mortal experience by relating it to the Eternal God in whom we live and move and have our being.

THE WHOLENESS OF THE CHURCH FOR THE WHOLENESS OF THE WORLD

The church truly catholic confesses Christ as Lord over the whole order of human *society*. She thereby accepts society as instituted by God. The family, the community, the nation, the assembly of the nations she sees as ordained by the divine will. "For there is no authority except from God, and those that exist have been instituted by God" (Rom. 13.1). This is not to say that every particular government is good, but that the order of government (like that of the family) is necessary for the fulfillment of the divine intent and thereby falls within the purview of her proper concern. So also with the orders of labor, of business, of recreation, of education.

The church truly catholic confesses Christ as Lord over the whole order of human *history*. She thereby accepts history and sees in the vast events of our time, in the struggles of men for justice and a fuller life, the moving of the divine purpose. So Julia Ward Howe, wrote a century ago in "The Battle Hymn of the Republic."

> I have seen Him in the watch-fires of a hundred circling camps;
> They have builded Him an altar in the evening dews and damps;
> I can read His righteous sentence by the dim and flaring lamps.
> > His day is marching on.

The church involves herself in the full sweep of human concerns on the stage of history.

Amid the revolutionary changes of our day, the church does not stand wringing her hands and longing for the old securities. Rather she asks what the Lord of history is saying to his church in these events and how she may respond to him in glad obedience. She knows that the social and cultural factors in the human situation have theological significance. In short, the church truly catholic is thoroughly and wholesomely secular. She manifests the holy worldliness to which Dietrich Bonhoeffer points us.

The church truly catholic confesses Christ as Lord over the whole order of human *culture* and thereby accepts as her concern all

151

of man's cultural life, past and present. As the early Christians moved out into the ancient world the issue soon confronted them: What were they to do with the inheritance of classical civilization? Because it was connected with the paganism which they had rejected, some Christians held that the culture also must be repudiated. But those of broader (more catholic) disposition saw a greater vision. All this was to be brought into captivity to Christ. So the ancient literature was claimed: "Whatever has been well said among all men belongs to us Christians." [1] The classical philosophers were hailed for having lived the life of reason, life with the Logos; thus, for all their limitations, they received a kind of justification. They were almost Christians before Christ, and their work was to be taken seriously, even though in itself it could not bestow salvation. [2]

Ever since the collapse of antique culture under the impact of the barbarian invasions, the church has been deeply involved in higher education—in the monasteries, the cathedral schools, the medieval universities, the Puritan academies, the "log-colleges" on the American frontier, the Christian liberal arts college and university, the institutions of learning established wherever Christian missionaries have gone. (In the massive enterprise which higher education has become in our contemporary culture the church lacks the financial resources to sustain any large part of it, but she rightfully recognizes the whole venture as one in which she has had a major role from the fall of Rome to the present.)

As for the creative arts, the church truly catholic has an obligation both to sustain the artist's vision and to ponder it herself as she seeks to understand and to minister to the human condition. For many centuries the church was the chief patron of the arts, especially during the Middle Ages and the Renaissance. Because of its break with the sensuous appeal of medieval worship and its supreme reliance upon the Word, reformed Protestantism virtually cut itself off from any living relationship with the creative arts. (Rembrandt is the one great exception, and he was not helped by the church.)

Because of the frontier heritage of American religion, the emotional tone of revivalism, and the somewhat sentimental character of the prevailing pietism, the churches of the United States have until recent years given almost no encouragement to the arts. Especially have they been slow to commission works in the contemporary idiom. In recent years, however, welcome changes are taking place. First in church architecture, then in the related arts of stained glass, the fashioning of altarware, and sculpture, much work is being done, some of it fresh and compelling in its authentically modern presentation of the gospel. The Lutheran churches have been notable in their encouragement of a renaissance of Christian art on both sides of the Atlantic.

The church truly catholic confesses Christ as Lord over the whole *order of powers that shape human destiny*. The church thereby finds herself engaged in her battle with the "powers." In Colossians we read the words the ancients used for the forces that mold man's life: "thrones or dominions or principalities or authorities" (Col. 1:16). Perhaps it is more modern—we seem to think that it is—to say " 'economic determinism' or 'dialectical materialism' or 'behavior patterns' or 'complexes.' " [3] Men all about us bow down to impersonal forces like heredity, environment, the business cycle, the cold war. But Christ is Lord over all the powers; it is by him that they exist. To the degree that they are subject to his lordship, the church accepts them; otherwise, she looks to his ultimate triumph over them.

The church who knows herself to be truly catholic then acknowledges as the realm of Christ's lordship the entire cosmos. She accepts the whole order of creation, of life, of society, of history, of culture. Only so can she avoid an irrelevant religiosity, lost in the mists of so-called spirituality. I confess that frequently after extended discussions on fine points of dogma at the seminary, or the reading of several religious books in a row, I become "fed up" for the time being with theology. It then proves refreshing and utterly wholesome to lose myself for a while in *Time,* or *Saturday Review* or the *American Historical Review,* where the full pageant of human life is spread out in all its vivid *this*-worldliness. For the church catholic teaches that we cannot live by theoretical abstractions nor can we find the God and Father of Jesus Christ by withdrawing from mundane affairs. The calling of the church is rather to be in the world through the daily life and work of all its members because it is God's, and we serve him by involving ourselves in it.

III

But does the church dare to identify herself with the world as completely as all this would indicate? "Is not this to secularize the Christian faith?" some will ask, who cling to the pietistic tradition of withdrawal from the world and from this-worldly concerns. "Is this not to sell out to the world?" others will demand, who retain the prophetic (and classical Protestant) conception of the world as under the judgment of God. "How," these latter will insist, "can we avoid making Christianity a mere culture-religion, a sort of court chaplain to the American Way of Life?"

The latter group of prophetic questions desperately requires to be put in our society where the natural tendency is to identify the will of God with the secularly-determined purposes of the community. Will Herberg and Martin Marty, to name only two recent authors, have demonstrated that most Americans, while professing to be religious, have no real sense of divine judgment calling into serious question any aspect of our life as the "good people" of our communities.[4] Our prevailing practice in personal morality, in race relations, in a society whose end seems to be only more and more consumption, in international affairs—in short, whatever we do—is held to be essentially in accord with the divine will and to merit divine favor. Ours is "a packaged God." We worship him, but worship is considered a means of invoking heavenly blessings on human undertakings entered into without serious effort to determine the will of God. Not only do we arrange prayers at stately public functions like the inauguration of a president or the opening of a legislature, but we also provide solemn invocations for such spectacles as college football games. What does this mean? That we confess all of life to be lived under the sovereignty of God and constantly open to his judgment? Or that we are simply presuming to invoke the sanctions of the Almighty in support of any and every enterprise of the all-virtuous Americans?

The crux of the issue is the lordship of Christ. Once we acknowledge him King of kings and Lord of lords, we can never presume on his easy favor for anything that we undertake. For whenever he confronts us it is in judgment and in mercy. We do not ask him to behold or to bless anything in which we are engaged until every aspect of the enterprise is submitted to the most searching examination by his all-seeing eyes. The radical secularity which we have been discussing then carries no indication whatever of an assumed divine approval for any man or any human venture. To confess Jesus Christ as Lord means to bow before him as Judge.

But the confession of his lordship also implies acknowledgement of the proper extent of his sovereignty, and that includes the whole cosmos. To speak as we have done therefore regarding the secular concern of the church is to indicate the vast domain of Christ's rule and the comparable extent of the church's mission. She must truly care for this entire scope of the world's life because in all these areas she knows that Christ must rule. The church catholic is involved with the whole world because she confesses Christ as Lord of all.

IV

Hence the need for the church's wholeness, for her constant eagerness to receive from her Lord a fuller measure of catholicity in her earthly life. For the church must present herself *in her wholeness* to the whole world of human concern. Catholicity is the condition of mission. How can a church which is willing to think of herself and her life as fractured bear any meaningful witness to the world in its totality, a world desperately in need of wholeness? Hence the importance of the ancient catholic movement (already alluded to) in the church of the first four centuries. Within (and to some degree beyond) the "one world" of the Roman empire, which was threatened by many divisive forces, the church sought to manifest itself as one. After the collapse of Roman rule and amidst the divisive tendencies of feudal Europe, the church in the West achieved impressive institutional unity, though in the form of an autocratic feudal monarchy. Even after the Reformation, several "national" churches retained integrity within the borders of their own states. But again these churches showed a tendency toward political and economic conservatism, a concern for their special prerogatives, the sin of self-preoccupation. It is never easy for the church to remember that her calling is not to be served but to serve, not to lord it over mankind but to give herself, not to expect society to do her work but to infuse the common life with the Christian witness and the Christian spirit.

Where the denominational form of Protestantism came to prevail, in England and especially in America, there was no wholeness of the church to pose against the concerns of the whole world. But there was still a profound recognition of Christ's lordship, which showed itself in the many voluntary societies formed in the nineteenth century to do the work of missions, evangelism, and social witness. Winthrop S. Hudson argues that these small associations of committed Christians who knew themselves to be a minority exercised a more profound influence over American life than the more prosperous, larger churches of later generations which have lost their sense of distinctiveness within the society.[5] He registers an important point. Mere bigness does not assure effective Christian witness. Nor can the church meaningfully proclaim the lordship of Christ over the world if it has become conformed to mundane standards.

But *wholeness* is needed. The purpose is not to exercise power but to manifest oneness, to overcome the irrelevance of denominational distinctions in the face of the world's need. A measure of such wholeness has been realized in the National Council of Churches and in the state councils. But their witness is in large measure vitiated by the insistence of the member churches that the council is not the church; thus its pronouncements lose the transcendent quality they might possess if spoken by a true church in the name of its Lord who is also Lord of the world, and they tend to become expressions of opinion from one of the many organizations pursuing its special interests within society.

Equally damaging is the sense of distance between the council and the average church member. He has some genuine sense of belonging not only to his congregation but to his denomination; he does not feel that he belongs in the same way to the state council or national council. The readiness of many earnest laymen to accept the ridiculous charges advanced in attacks upon the National Council of Churches, or their failure to be outraged by these as they would be by similar attacks upon their own denominations, indicate the sense of distance. The councils are about as close to the typical member as second cousins once removed: There is a connection, but he does not see it as meaning much. The causes which the councils serve so sincerely but still insufficiently need to find more adequate expression in genuine churchly life.

V

The implications for the movement toward Christian unity are apparent. The closing of every breach in the house of God restores a greater measure of wholeness to its mission. The efforts of the Consultation on Church Union to move toward a reunited church truly catholic, truly reformed, truly evangelical thus become invested with profound importance. The really significant aspect of such a church, if it should be achieved by the union of the six participating denominations, would not be her size as a power bloc of twenty million members within the national life. The calling of the church is not "to throw her weight around." Her real significance would be in the larger measure of wholeness than any of our separate communions has been able to bring to our mission to the world.

Here would be a truly national church, represented with strength in every part of the United States. It has been suggested that there would be scarcely a village in America which would not have a congregation of the reunited church.[6] In thousands of communities the opportunity would be presented, as soon as local opinion was ready, for the union of weak and insufficient congregations now related to two or more of the denominations involved. Much of the fracturing of the common life which the church has brought about would thus be redeemed. The church would contribute in a much more significant way than ever before to the integrity of local communities. Far more realistically than any of the denominations has been able to do, the church would be able to assess her responsibility to villages and cities, to the various states, and to the nation as a whole. Here would be a church fit for these times, a manifestation of the reconciling power which is in Christ, of the wholeness which his grace provides for a broken and distraught world.

It must be repeated that catholicity is not merely—or even primarily—a matter of bigness or of greater political influence as a power bloc. The wholeness of a reunited church is a realization of the integrating effectiveness of divine grace, its capacity to hold together the diverse components of life, to invest them with sanctity and meaning.

The church should know from her own sacraments that God has given her wholeness to be used for the sake of the world. The most sacred moment of her worship, when her unity is most intensely realized, is radically secular. Many Christians, on coming to worship, pray that all thoughts of daily affairs may be put aside. They are mistaken. In the words of institution for the Lord's supper, we are told that "Jesus took bread." One can get no closer to the world than that. Bread is the product of man's plowing, sowing, waiting, harvesting, threshing, milling, baking, selling, buying. It can come only from man's life in the world. It is not spiritual; it is worldly. The holy table is not a refuge from the reality of life, not a denial of the world. It is the place where God reveals his involvement in the world, as Creator, Judge, Immanuel, Redeemer, Lord. All its concerns belong here. As Christians we come to the table with no less of the world upon us than is upon any other human beings, but rather with more. Here we know what it is to live in the world by divine grace and under the lordship of Christ. From the table we go forth with a renewed vision of life made whole, and we take up our work for the wholeness of the world.[7]

A church fit for these times must possess the wholeness of catholicity, not only as expressed in reunited institution but as made manifest in the sacraments. It is instructive to reflect upon the contribution of the Christian faith to those creative artists who have been able to relate the witness of the gospel to the deepest problems of mankind through their art. Those churches which claim for themselves the catholic tradition (Orthodox, Roman, Anglican) have produced a company of great creative poets, dramatists, and novelists from Dante to Dostoevski to Eliot to Pasternak. Other notable members of such a company among the writers of our own time are C. S. Lewis, Dorothy Sayers, Christopher Fry, Graham Greene. These are all laymen. None of them is a professional theologian or even a clergyman. Yet their insight into the human condition and their knowledge of the Christian faith are such that they have been able through genuine works of art, not sermons in crude artistic form, to suggest the wholeness of the gospel. (It is striking that few Protestants can be called to mind who deserve a place in such a company.)

One of the most imperative needs of the church catholic is to develop among her members a profound knowledge of the Christian faith, both in mind and in heart. Disciples so equipped may carry into the various vocations and responsibilities of contemporary society the kind of insights represented by these authors at their best. It is my conviction that only a church of true integrity, a church which manifests authentic wholeness in her own life, a church with a vital tradition, a church which gladly accepts the full sweep of Christ's lordship, can adequately prepare her members for this sort of witness. Thus wholeness for the church is essential for her mission of bringing wholeness to the world.

VI

One of the most daring—we must almost say presumptuous—reaches of biblical thought sees the wholeness of the church as a manifestation of God's intent for all mankind, a redeemed humanity under the lordship of Christ.

The divine purpose is clearly expressed in Col. 1:20: "to reconcile to himself all things." The following verses see that purpose as already fulfilled within the church: "You, who once were estranged and hostile . . . he has now reconciled." Here is the catholic community of those who know the divine intent for all mankind, who have heard it through the preaching of the gospel, and who already show forth in the quality of their common life the purpose of God for all his children.

A dramatic picture of this concept appears in Paul's letter to the Philippians where he asserts that "our commonwealth is in heaven (Phil. 3:20). In James Moffatt's vivid rendition of this passage, "We are a colony of heaven."

Here on the bleak shores of human existence God has planted an outpost of his people. We must live the life of this earth as fully as we are able, learning to use the resources of this land where we have been settled to make a better way of life for ourselves and for our children. But as colonists we are not only newcomers in a strange land; we are citizens of the home country. (In ancient times Greek colonists carried with them from their mother-city a sacred flame from its altar and a quantity of their native soil. The English settlers who came to America brought with them a great tradition of "laws, freedom, truth, and faith in God." From this came one of the great differences between the culture of the Indians which the English settlers supplanted and that which they established, making use of the same natural resources.) The church catholic, sent into the world as a colony of heaven, takes the world just as seriously as anyone living in it, but brings to it something new—a high tradition, a sense of ultimate purpose, a commitment to the lordship of Christ.

The tendency of our American denominations, taken as a whole or in individual communities, has been to identify with particular elements in society.[8] Each has become to some degree a "class church," thus denying to that extent the divine purpose of bringing all things to oneness in Christ. A church truly catholic will, by the grace of God, transcend this kind of social distinction and show forth in her own life the power of the gospel to achieve a community of the reconciled.

An honest consideration of the issues faced in this chapter cannot leave any Christian or any denomination feeling comfortable in the face of our ecclesiastical life as it now is in America. But the will of God for his church as the reconciled and reconciling people is becoming increasingly clear. What man in his perversity and ignorance cannot achieve on his own the Lord of the church can give by his grace. It now begins to appear that in the divine providence the time may be ripe for the achievement within the reformation tradition of a church truly catholic in a sense far deeper than has been known before. Such a gift must be a cause for great rejoicing, but more: for renewed consecration to mission. For the wholeness of the church is for the wholeness of the world.

PART V

An Appeal for Faithful Obedience

CHAPTER 10
Move We On Together

Leaders in the ecumenical movement frequently engage in sly humor at their own expense. This is a good sign, for while they are seriously committed to their cause, it is important that they should not take themselves too seriously. One wry bit going about at Montreal during the Fourth World Conference on Faith and Order in 1963 reported what the Gadarene swine allegedly said to one another as they rushed toward the edge of the precipice above the sea: "We must keep moving and we must all stay together."

The relish with which this story is told in ecumenical circles indicates full awareness of the limitations of our most popular slogans. Unity for its own sake may not necessarily be of significant value. And all rapid movement is not necessarily progress. Anyone who has read this book even casually has found these truths reiterated. There is no real point, and there are dangers in seeking a united church just for the sake of bigness or purely in the interest of change. But the existence of wrong reasons does not invalidate right reasons. The latter are suggested in the well-known hymn, "Forward through the Ages" by Frederick Lucian Hosmer:

> Bound by God's far purpose
> In one living whole,
> Move we on together
> To the shining goal!

It is my conviction that God purposes a church sufficient for these times to a degree far exceeding the present achievement of our divided denominations. Such a church will transcend many of our present denominational separations, which are understandable enough in the historic context of their origins, but without significance or integrity in the contemporary world. God will give his faithful people the ability to transcend the limitations imposed by their past as they respond in fuller obedience to his will. Certainly much of his will for his church is suggested in the phrases we have examined—"truly evangelical, truly reformed, truly catholic."

If the crucial weakness of the church in our time is introversion, her life turned in upon herself, it might have seemed more appropriate to have written this book about the needs of the world. Get the church's mind off herself and onto the area of needed service. But we cannot and ought not to dispense with the church. The church is the body of Christ to do his work among men. And she is hampered in this work today by the forms of institutional life inherited from another and quite different culture. Only as we change these self-consciously to give us a church for these times can she be free to carry out her mission.

This book is written out of a lifelong love for the church to men and women who have responded to the call of Christ as Lord. It is my belief that he has summoned us to live and serve through his church and that the rightful work of the church is both necessary and significant to the welfare of our society. I confess that the church as we know her in America falls far short of the divine intention for her. But I am convinced that the time has come to chart a course. We must go beyond self-criticism to action, the action of obedience to Christ as Lord.

It would be presumptuous at this point to suggest that Christ's will for his church will be to accept whatever proposals may issue in due time from the Consultation on Church Union. We, can affirm, however, with deep conviction and certainty, that our Lord's intention for his church in America includes a much fuller realization of her churchly nature—evangelical, reformed, and catholic—than she now manifests in her institutional life. Two necessary corollaries follow: (*a*) the explorations in which the Consultation is engaged are of the greatest importance for all the churches in the United States, and (*b*) the issues implicit in the mandate laid upon the Consultation deserve the most prayerful and thoughtful consideration of the members of the communions directly involved.

I

No one should imagine that I have undertaken in the nine brief chapters of this book to solve all the problems which must be worked out if the Consultation is to offer a plan of union acceptable to the churches concerned. I have not even attempted to suggest what all the problems are because I am convinced that *to begin with the problems is to start wrong-end-to!*

The moment a proposal for union is suggested, our natural human inclination is to respond, "But what about . . . ?" The problem indicated may be apostolic succession, episcopal ordination, the form of baptism, the frequency of holy communion, liturgy, creeds, church government, or what you will. (In all conscience, would it not be more accurate to conclude, "or what you will *not*"?)

167

I am convinced that workable solutions to these problems are available, solutions which are theologically valid and which should be convincing to the most sensitive conscience. We owe the possibility of such solutions to the hard-working biblical scholars, theologians, and church historians of all communions throughout the world, and particularly to the common ecumenical experience of the past half-century. I have not attempted to advance my own solutions to many of these problems, for the fundamental principles which must be employed are widely known. And it is important in the Consultation on Church Union that answers emerge as a consensus of those participating, rather than appear as a platform written by one or two persons.

But solutions will be given only as we see the problems in the perspective of God's will for his church. To begin with particular issues is to raise the weary old questions in the same old way, so that we flail all the old chaff over again and find very few kernels of new truth. Therefore I have not been concerned to provide in this book an outline for the study of all the problems. What I have hoped to do is to enlist the readers in a serious attempt to discern afresh the purpose of God for his church in our times and to suggest how that purpose may be much more fully realized through the type of church which the Consultation on Church Union has been asked to explore. Only within a new and fuller understanding of the nature of the church in God's design will the Christian people of America be able to face constructively the problems which will arise and to accept the answers which may be forthcoming. Unless we see the church in the light of the gospel and of the lordship of Christ, there is no hope.

Whether or not the Consultation on Church Union will succeed in finding a basis for the reunion of the United Presbyterian Church, the Protestant Episcopal Church, The Methodist Church, the United Church of Christ, the Evangelical United Brethren, and the Christian Churches (Disciples of Christ), no one can now say. The ecumenical era has been an age of miracles, and doubtless the Lord and Head of the church still has some in store for his faithful people. A particular program for union may fail. But we believe that the fulfillment of God's will for the life of his church must move along the main lines which this book has sought to describe. If the members of the six communions involved can place the divine intention for the church above loyalty to their particular traditions, reunion is a genuine possibility.

With the same sense of earnestness which marked the "Plea to American Christians" at the start, I now conclude this book. In doing so, I wish to address a number of persons quite directly. Please find your place or places in the following paragraphs.

Every Church Member in the Six Churches

It is only through you that the will of Christ can be made effective in this matter. For humanly speaking, all six of the churches concerned are governed (directly or indirectly) by their members. The common understanding and the common obedience to the Lord's will are the decisive factors.

Then let your impatience with the present denominational situation be known. Speak out concerning your commitment to a church sufficient for these times. Encourage your minister with the knowledge that you and many other church members are ready for such a reformation of our present ecclesiastical structure as Christ wills. Write letters to the editors of your denominational papers concerning the need for a reunited church, not just a bigger organization but a church truly evangelical, reformed, catholic. Study these matters in groups within your congregation and discuss them informally.[1] Prepare yourself with theological understanding and with pertinent facts, so that when fearful Committeesto-Preserve-Our-Dear-Old-Denomination-Just-As-It-Always-Was-Forever-and-Ever-Amen are organized you will not be swept off your feet by thoughtless charges, frantic drumbeating, and the emotional repetition of ancient slogans.

You should know that a great host of ministers and of denominational officials long for a reunited church. They are ready for it right now. But they have been taught the myth that their members are opposed to church union, and they do not want to stir up trouble. Let them know that as one church member you are ready for a far greater church than any to which you have ever been privileged to belong. And let them know that many other members feel just as you do.

Every Young Person in the Six Churches

Perhaps no generation of Christians since the Protestant Reformation has stood in such a fateful position as your own. For it is quite possible that in your lifetime—and before the passage of many more years—you and your fellow Christians will be deciding for or against a reunited Church. Obviously the six communions involved are still a minority within Protestantism, but they constitute a very significant part of it. And if these six can find their way toward realization of a church truly evangelical, reformed, catholic, surely others will also move toward participation.

You are in a highly favored position. For you have grown up in the ecumenical era. You love the church. You thrill to her heritage. You are loyal to her work. But you have seen for yourself that the life of any one denomination is tragically partial. You know that the common witness of Christian young people in your school is shattered by denominational division. You are grateful to your home church and to your own tradition, but you know that there is no sound reason to keep your particular denomination alive forever. Your commitment is to Jesus Christ and to his great church.

170

Many adults hold to the myth that young people have no serious interest in the church, that you just want to be entertained. Let your minister, your parents, your leaders know what you feel about the kind of church in which you want to spend your life. Do not start a rebellion. Do not antagonize. But make your commitment to the goal of a reunited church known. And as you ponder what you will do with your life, ask God to use you in helping the Christian people of America to achieve such a goal. Perhaps you are needed as a minister to help lead in this great venture. Perhaps your place is as a faithful, well-informed member seeking to respond obediently to God so that the church of A.D. 2000 may be fit for the times.

Every Minister in the Six Churches

You have given your life to the ministry of reconciliation and you love the church. Yet you know more than anyone else the failures, insufficiencies, and (at least) mild hypocrisies of the denominational system. Unless you are different from most of your colleagues, you did not enter the ministry because of a passion to promote the particular doctrines or to build up the institutions of your own denomination. Your motivation was a readiness to serve God and man, out of deep love for both, through the church. Do you remember the high vision of Christlike ministry with which you responded to the call of God?

You have found deep satisfaction in the ministry. But you have also found it a man-killing job. Anyone trying to minister to several hundred persons in the spirit of Christ has all he can do. Add to that the labor of keeping up the organizational life of a modern congregation. Add preparation for worship, for preaching, for the many other addresses and lessons you are called on to present. Add the demands made by your denomination for its general work. Add the claims of your community and of the council of churches.

171

Throw in the special problems in your own situation—those members of the Perennial Opposition, the suspicion of your position on social issues, the diehard loyalty to the peculiarities of the denomination, and any others which come to mind. All this adds up to a situation in which it may be just a little too easy to leave things as they are. You may have asked yourself whether you have the time and the energy to lead your people through the many discussions (perhaps controversies) and difficult adjustments of a move toward a reunited church.

If it were already here you would be grateful. You would much rather serve in a church truly evangelical, reformed, catholic. You deeply appreciate the particular heritage of your own communion and the forms in which the grace of God has come to you. But your real interest is not in proclaiming your denominational peculiarities. You have not lived and prayed through the ecumenical era for nothing. But you just are not sure that anyone else is as concerned about a united church as you are.

Then remember this. Millions of church members are ready for a united church. They have proved it by their votes with their church letters; when they move from one community to another most of them unite with some congregation in their new location, but with little concern for staying in the same denomination. While they may not be able to state their position in the theological language that is now in vogue, their common sense tells them that our denominational divisions are foolish, wasteful, and irrelevant. Such loyalty as they now devote to their denomination and its peculiar witness they have learned from you or your predecessors. And perhaps you have not shared with them sufficiently the fruits of the fuller scholarship of our ecumenical era. It is a sad commentary that still in the 1960's too many laymen, to whom the idea of a united church makes sense, have guilt feelings about unfaithfulness to some denominational peculiarity. Even so, they long to do the will of Christ.

Our church members are ready for a reunited church, or are ready to begin facing the issue. But they have been beguiled by the myth that the ministers are not interested. Because they see you carrying out your ministry according to the peculiar forms and practices of your denomination—there is scarcely any other way to do it unless you change denominations—they assume that these peculiarities mean a great deal to you. Since you have received a professional theological education they further presume that there are weighty reasons, not apparent to them, why you will probably not welcome any suggestions for change in the church. But once they get over the shock of having these illusions dispelled, they are ready for you to exercise leadership toward a church fit for these times. No such great movement is likely to come without your open commitment to it.

Every Seminarian in the Six Churches

You are searching. Unlike your predecessors in some earlier generations you have not entered on study for the ministry with great dogmatic convictions. You are puzzled about your own life, about the world, about God. You do not know what to think about the church. But you are seeking answers. And you believe that they may be found within the community of faith, if only you can see things freshly and honestly.

You have been exposed to an unconscionable amount of criticism directed at the church, her life, her theology, her ministry, her understanding of her mission. Much of this criticism has been justified. Yet even honest and accurate self-criticism can become self-destructive, however well-intended. Signs abound that the constant reiteration of the weaknesses in the church seriously threatens her morale. Many ministers are depressed in spirit. Young people brought up on a diet of analysis have not been moved in large numbers to give themselves to the service of such a church. Laymen are hardly encouraged by being told that their devotion really makes no difference in the major issues confronting our world.

The time has come to move beyond negatives. The ministry of the next thirty years will in large measure determine whether the churches remain in the impotence and irrelevance of their denominational separation or whether they respond to the will of God concerning a church sufficient for these times. Your ministry is set in a fateful day.

You have untold advantages. Yours is the first generation of ministers to have received its education under the full impact of the ecumenical reformation. The real work you have done in biblical studies, in theology, in church history, has been in no sense sectarian. And although you may not realize it, this is a new situation. The churches to which you will minister, while perhaps weighted with denominational traditions, have been exposed somewhat to the ecumenical climate, and many are ready for a new day.

Your work will require patience. And more than any other seminarian of this century, you will have to struggle for the gift of vivid and concrete expression. So much of the discipline of our seminaries in this past decade has lifted students into the stratosphere of abstract terminology. But in the years immediately ahead you may have the glorious opportunity of translating the insights of the first half-century of ecumenical thought into reality in the life of the church. If you work faithfully, you may be granted the privilege of spending a large part of your ministry within a reunited church.

Every Official in the Six Churches

You have your hands full. Because you have proven your effectiveness in church work and especially your creativity in projecting significant programs you have been called to your present post. You

174

are overworked. You are constantly burdened by a multitude of pressing responsibilities and harassed by new and rapidly breaking crises. It is all you can do to keep your head above water. Yet you love the church. You believe in her mission. You long for opportunity for study and reflection, but your wish is only rarely granted. Still you press on in your service, hoping to carry out your assignment and to advance the witness of the church.

You are under no illusion that Christianity in twentieth-century America can dispense with institution, even though you wish you could devote more of your energy to pastoral concern for persons and to other spiritual pursuits. You are a realist and you accept the necessity of working within the denominational system. You know that your denomination functions primarily as an operational unit (more or less effective) within the total Christian enterprise and only to a far lesser degree as a witness to some peculiar truths or emphases within its historic tradition. Because you are a realist you know that the perpetuation of denominations in their present form is neither the most expeditious way of conducting the Christian mission in our time nor of serving the special emphases in their traditions. While you may shudder at the prospect of the labor needed to work out a major reunion among our churches, you know that a reunited church would provide a far more meaningful and effective means of Christian service.

You also know (though many persons are not aware that you know it) that millions of laymen and thousands of ministers are ready for a reunited church. But they have accepted the myth that you are blind to their concern and that you oppose reunion because of your vested interest in your job. They have let themselves believe that you are the defender of the denominational *status quo* in order to preserve your present position of leadership. This widely accepted myth is without foundation. To one who has worked closely with the ecumenical movement it is well known that throughout the

175

much maligned "hierarchies" and "bureaucracies" of our denominations, at every level is a host of dedicated Christian men and women committed to the will of God for his church, eager for a larger degree of union, and already engaged in many unsung labors of cooperation and reconciliation. More than anyone else you know the intricate problems of organizational adjustment which must be worked out in case of union, and more than anyone else you are ready to work on them, even if—unlikely condition!—the achievement of a united church should mean a reduction in your own personal status and influence.

But there is more which must be done. The realization of such a church awaits prophetic leadership and it must come from men in positions like yours in every echelon of our denominational institutions. It is by now a truism that the early heroes of the ecumenical movement were "charismatic" rather than "official" leaders. They pioneered in the cause of reconciliation. It is witness both to their vision and to their achievement that they were able to involve the churches *officially* in the ecumenical enterprise. So, as has frequently been said, leadership passed from the prophets to the priests. That is no loss. It is the only way that religious gains are ever conserved; they must be built into the life of the institution. And yet, many a man in your position, it must be admitted, carries his ecumenical responsibilities as perfunctory duties, a few of the chores of his office among a very great many. In some instances what began as prophecy now appears as stale routine.

It will not do to romanticize the iconoclast and the outsider. The gains to be made in our time must come responsibly, through the "power structure," if we are to receive a church truly evangelical, reformed, catholic, in its fullest sense. And for that to happen the torch of ecumenical prophecy must be raised again by men like yourself and your colleagues. It is not enough to take your turn in the honorific offices or even the hard-working chairmanships in councils of churches and world conferences held in exotic settings. The weight of your influence and your position must be registered as dramatically as possible on behalf of a church sufficient to these times.

It is heartening that the chain of incidents which launched the Consultation on Church Union was set in motion by the "chief bureaucrat"—to use an often pejorative term in a nonpejorative sense—of one denomination with the assistance of a bishop in another communion. A large part of the effective leadership of the Consultation has been provided by bureaucrats—bishops and state secretaries, agency presidents and board secretaries, seminary presidents and deans—as well as by pastors and laymen. For the effort to get much beyond its present stage, you and others like you in each of the denominations involved must go to work in your own sphere of influence, as considerations of timeliness warrant. Under the leadership of our state executive, for example, the Commission on Ecumenical Relations of my own denomination in my state has already launched a program of study among our church leaders and has authorized appropriate approaches to the officials of the five other participating communions concerning the feasibility of some common study. No war is won without resourceful, determined, and committed captains and generals.

Every Outsider Beyond the Organized Church

If you have read to this point, I am grateful for your concern. I cannot speculate here on all the reasons why you have chosen to remain outside the institutional life of the Christian community. You must have some regard for the church or you would not have followed thus far. Perhaps you honor the Christian heritage of our Western culture, even though for reasons satisfactory to yourself you remain detached from the institution. Nevertheless you regard it not unappreciatively as part of your heritage as a Western man.

Yet for all your aloofness, such a man as yourself exerts a real influence on the church.

The heart of Frankfurt, Germany, was obliterated by the Allied bombers in World War II. Within that ancient city today you find yourself surrounded by acres of modernistic aluminum and glass buildings, an island of contemporaneity girdled by residential structures from centuries long previous. Yet almost in the center of this mid-twentieth century island looms the medieval church of St. Katherine. How did it survive in that incongruous setting? It was no miracle. The ancient church was leveled by the bombs, just like the other buildings all around it. But it was piously rebuilt stone upon stone, the one authentic memorial from the prewar city. It towers as a symbol of much popular understanding of the church —a landmark, a link with our racial past, a museum of ancestral piety, a monument to antiquity. Do you not commonly think of the church in such terms? And so you remain outside.

But if only you will enter the Church of St. Katherine you will be stunned by the modernity of the interior. The medieval glass and ecclesiastical art could hardly have been reduplicated. The great nave is flooded with light filtered through stained glass in the modern idiom. The altar and other appointments are equally contemporary in their mode of presenting the ancient gospel. For all its external appearances, this is obviously a living church.

If you will take the trouble to "get inside" the church in America today, the church at her best, you will find that she is stirring with new life. Movements of reform and renewal are at work for the strengthening of her spirit, the stirring up of her mind, and the stimulation of her energies to meaningful Christian mission in our time. Perhaps you have seen little evidence of these things. Perhaps then the fault is partly yours. If the church as you know her is still too largely a museum of antiquities, the cause may not be solely the inertia of its members. Perhaps you and many others like you have insisted that the proper role of the church in our society is to be guardian of the past, not a true participant in contemporary affairs. Perhaps the lack of relevance you feel in the church may derive from a role you have forced upon it.

In any case, look for the new life in the church. For it is life for you.

II

In conclusion here is one more brief address which is intended for a wide and responsible audience.

Every Christian in All the Churches

As a follower of Christ in the world today, whatever your denominational affiliation, you confess his lordship over the totality of human life. He has called his people to mission. An obedient church therefore must be concerned with the world, with all the crucial issues of the times. But she will face them, I am convinced, as the church of Jesus Christ, his body of believers called to serve mankind in these days. Even though therefore we are called for mission and must devote our prayers and concern to the world of human need, we must give attention to the life of the church. That is the justification for this book.

The great failure of the denomination has been its majoring in minors. The overemphasis on the lesser matters of the law has thus obscured the witness to the gospel and has hampered effectiveness in mission. One of the most devout and spiritually discerning leaders of the American nation was so repulsed by the partiality and irrelevance of the denominations in his day that he remained aloof from them. Abraham Lincoln's comment is well known:

I have never united myself to any church, because I have found difficulty in giving my assent, without mental reservation, to the long, compli-

179

cated statements of Christian doctrine which characterize their articles of belief and confessions of faith. When any church will inscribe over its altars, as its sole qualification for membership, the Savior's condensed statement of the substance of both law and gospel, "Thou shalt love the Lord thy God with all thy heart, and with all thy soul, and with all thy mind, and thy neighbor as thyself," that church will I join with all my heart and all my soul.[2]

Whether Lincoln's epitomizing of the essential character of the true church is completely acceptable or not, it has point for everyone who loves the church today. The wholeness of the church, her commitment to the central concerns of her Lord, her deliverance from pettiness and partiality are essential if she is to fulfill her calling in this hour. So all Christians must be concerned for a church truly evangelical, truly reformed, truly catholic. The next step in our obedience will not be the same for every believer in America. But all must be keenly sensitive and gladly responsive to the divine call. We must all pray for one another, for the whole company of God's people, and for every effort to acknowledge more fully the lordship of Christ over his church.

Prayer. Obedience. Faithfulness. Service. Mission. Joy. To these Christ calls his people. And to us who look to him he will give a church for these times.

A Prayer for the Church

O God, of unchangeable power and eternal light, look favorably on Thy whole Church, that wonderful and sacred mystery; and by the tranquil operation of Thy perpetual Providence, carry out the work of Man's salvation; and let the whole world feel and see that things which were cast down are being raised up, and things which had grown old are being made new, and all things are returning to perfection through Him through whom they took their origin; even through our Lord Jesus Christ.[3]

NOTES

Chapter 1

1 From "We Would be Building." Words copyright © 1936 by Purd E. Dietz. *Pilgrim Hymnal* (Boston: The Pilgrim Press, 1958), #494.

2 Anne Fremantle (ed.), "The Acts of the Scillitan Saints," in *A Treasury of Early Christianity* (New York: Viking Press, 1958), pp. 211-13.

3 "Canticles" (Song of Solomon) 3:1, *The Holy Bible—Old Testament, Douay Version* (New York: P. J. Kenedy & Sons, 1961).

4 J. H. Oldham, *The Churches Survey Their Task*, p. 82, quoted in Ruth Rouse and S. C. Neill (eds.), *A History of the Ecumenical Movement* (London: Westminster Press, 1954), p. 591.

5 Robert McAfee Brown and David H. Scott (eds.), *The Challenge to Reunion* (New York: McGraw-Hill, 1963), pp. 271, 275-76, 277-81.

6 Harold E. Fey, "Catholic, Reformed, Evangelical," *The Christian Century*, June 7, 1961, p. 702.

7 The most readily available discussions of the proposal are in the Reflection Book edited by George L. Hunt and Paul A. Crow, Jr., *Where We Are in Church Union* (New York: Association Press, 1965). See also *The Challenge to Reunion*, edited by Brown and Scott, and the *Digest of the Proceedings of the Consultation on Church Union for 1962 and 1963*, volumes I and II combined. Volume III (1964) is available as a separate issue.

Copies may be secured from the executive secretary, George L. Hunt, Box 69, Fanwood, New Jersey.

Chapter 3

1 John Milton, "Lycidas."

2 Oscar Cullmann, *Early Christian Worship,* trans. A. Stewart Todd and James B. Torrance ("Studies in Biblical Theology") [Chicago: Henry Regnery Company, 1953], p. 14.

3 Theodore Otto Wedel *et al., The Liturgical Renewal of the Church* (New York: Oxford University Press, 1960), p. 5.

4 John Rathbone Oliver, *Pastoral Psychiatry and Mental Health* (New York: Charles Scribner's Sons, 1932), pp. 162-63.

5 *The Interpreter's Bible* (Nashville: Abingdon Press, 1951), VII, 4.

6 Christopher Fry, *Thor, With Angels* (London: Oxford University Press, 1951), pp. 32-33, 40.

Chapter 4

1 Martin E. Marty, "Reformation Remembered," *The Christian Century,* December 4, 1963, pp. 1522-24, 1530.

2 Ph.-H. Menoud, "Holy Spirit," in J. J. von Allmen (ed.), *A Companion to the Bible* trans. P. J. Allcock and others (New York: Oxford University Press, 1958), p. 171.

3 *The Interpreter's Bible* (Nashville: Abingdon Press, 1951), VII, 746-53.

4 Particularly suggestive at this point is Günther Bornkamm, *Jesus of Nazareth,* trans. Irene and Fraser McLuskey (New York: Harper & Row, 1960), pp. 17-22, 25, 136, 191.

5 Ernst Käsemann, "Unity and Diversity in New Testament Ecclesiology," *Novum Testamentum,* VI, 296.

6 Hans Urs von Balthasar, *A Theology of History* (New York: Sheed and Ward, 1963), p. 103.

7 Brown and Scott, *The Challenge to Reunion,* p. 278.

Chapter 5

1 Winfred E. Garrison, *An American Religious Movement* (St. Louis: Bethany Press, 1945), p. 19.

2 Abraham Joshua Heschel, "Protestant Renewal: A Jewish View," *The Christian Century,* December 4, 1963, p. 1502.

3 G. G. Coulton, *Five Centuries of Religion* (New York: Cambridge University Press, 1923), I, 155.

4 John Greenleaf Whittier, "Our Master."

5 Edgar DeWitt Jones, *Fairhope: The Annals of a Country Church* (New York: The Macmillan Company, 1917), p. 35.

Chapter 6

1 D. M. Baillie, *God Was in Christ* (New York: Charles Scribner's Sons, 1948), p. 204.

2 Quoted in "Ecumenical Material on 'The Missionary Structure of the Congregation,'" *A Monthly Letter About Evangelism* (World Council of Churches), February, 1963, p. 1.

Chapter 7

1 Rouse and Neill, *A History of the Ecumenical Movement,* pp. 250-51, 264-65.

2 Alexander Campbell, *Christian Baptism: with its antecedents and consequents* (Bethany, Va., 1851), p. 18.

3 See Royal Humbert (ed.), *A Compend of Alexander Campbell's Theology* (St. Louis: Bethany Press, 1961), p. 266 for a very discerning critical footnote (#3) which should prove instructive to many Disciples concerning Campbell's attitude on creeds.

4 Alexander Campbell, *The Christian System in Reference to the Union of Christians and a Restoration of Primitive Christianity as Plead in the Current Reformation* (Pittsburgh: Forrester & Campbell, 1839), p. 10.

5 I do not propose to shape this discussion by the particular concerns of Disciples of Christ any more than the two which have preceded. However, may I mention in passing my concluding essay in *The Reformation of Tradition,* Volume I of the Panel of Scholars Reports (St. Louis: Bethany Press, 1963). There I have discussed the continuing witness of Disciples of Christ under the four rubrics: unity, apostolicity, holiness, and catholicity. I repeat here very little of what I wrote there, but I believe that material is, for Disciples, equally pertinent to a consideration of this theme.

6 Douglas Horton, *Congregationalism: A Study in Church Polity* (London: Independent Press Ltd., 1952).

7 Douglas Horton, *The United Church of Christ* (New York: Thomas Nelson & Sons, 1962), pp. 58-86.

Chapter 8

1 W. A. Visser 't Hooft (ed.), *New Delhi Speaks* (New York: Association Press, 1962), pp. 92-93.

2 Daniel Jenkins, *Congregationalism: a Restatement* (New York: Harper & Brothers, 1954), pp. 78 ff.

3 The denomination performs a paradoxical function within the church universal. While its existence is an obvious evidence of the brokenness of the body of Christ, it fulfills an important service as a (limited) instrument of catholicity. See my paper "The Role of the Denomination," *Encounter,* XXII (1961), 160-74.

4 Brown and Scott, *The Challenge to Reunion,* p. 275.

5 For a discussion of the catholicity of councils of churches, see my paper "The Church of Christ, the Denomination, and the Council of Churches," *Encounter,* XX (1959), 72-93.

6 Claude Welch, "Catholicity," Fourth World Conference on Faith and Order, July 6, 1963. Stenciled copy, pp. 5-6.

7 Archpriest Vitali Borovoy, "Meaning of Catholicity," Fourth World Conference on Faith and Order, July 6, 1963. Stenciled copy, pp. 6, 8.

Chapter 9

1 Justin Martyr, *Second Apology,* XIII.

2 Clement of Alexandria, *Stromateis.*

3 *The Interpreter's Bible* (Nashville: Abingdon Press, 1955), XI, 161.

4 Will Herberg, *Protestant-Catholic-Jew* (New York: Doubleday & Company, 1955); and Martin E. Marty, *The New Shape of American Religion* (New York: Harper & Row, 1959).

5 Winthrop S. Hudson, *The Great Tradition of the American Churches* (New York: Torchbooks; Harper & Brothers, 1953)

6 George G. Beazley, Jr., "Beazley Buzz," *News on Christian Unity,* III, (April, 1963), 2.

7 I have developed this thought in a communion meditation "Bread of the World," *The Pulpit,* May, 1964, p. 152.

8 H. Richard Niebuhr, *The Social Sources of Denominationalism* (Cleveland: Meridian Books, 1929). Vance Packard, *The Status Seekers* (New York: Pocket Books, Inc., 1961), Ch. 14.

Chapter 10

1 Wide use should be made in study groups of *Where We Are in Church Union,* edited by Hunt and Crow.

2 Edgar Dewitt Jones, *Lincoln and the Preachers* (New York: Harper & Brothers, 1948), p. 141.

3 Gelasian Sacramentary, quoted in Robert N. Rodenmayer (ed), *The Pastor's Prayerbook* (New York: Oxford University Press, 1960), p. 169.

1 "Are 'developed' nations through their transnational institutions 'ahead' in the World", The Futurist, 1968, p. 152.

5 H. Richard Niebuhr, in *Social Sources of Denominationalism* (Cleveland: Meridian Books, 1929; New York: Henry Holt, 1929, New York: World Pocket Books, 1957), Ch. III.

Chapter 10

1 "What else should be made to study groups of liberals like an album?" from a letter by Huntington Cairns.

2 Peter Drucker, *The Age of Discontinuity* (New York: Harper Brothers, 1968), p. 18.

3 Chaucer, *Sir Thopas*, quoted in Robert K. Redmayne (ed.), *The Oxford Dictionary of Nursery Rhymes* (Oxford: Oxford University Press, 1960), p. 102.

INDEX

188

INDEX OF SCRIPTURE

192

D

INDEX OF SCRIPTURE

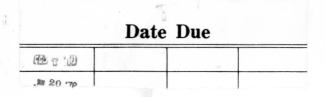